ECONOMIC VALUE OF CHILDREN AND FERTILITY

By

D. Usha Rani, K. Venkatesh Babu
and
M.V. Sudhakara Reddy

Sri Venkateswara University
Tirupati, (A.P), India.

2003

DISCOVERY PUBLISHING HOUSE
NEW DELHI–110002

First Published-2003

ISBN 81-7141-651-9

Published by

DISCOVERY PUBLISHING HOUSE
4831/24, Ansari Road, Prahlad Street,
Darya Ganj, New Delhi-110002 (India)
Phone: 3279245 • Fax: 91-11-3253475
E-mail:dphtemp@indiatimes.com

Printed at:
Arora Offset Press
Laxmi Nagar, Delhi 110 092.

Contents

Preface

India exhibits substantial variations and differentials in reproductive preferences and demographic behaviour. One major factor that underlies the reproductive preferences of Indians is the economic value of children. The value of children is a new research area, very important in the general area of determinants of fertility particularly micro level determinants. Value of children is not the exclusive domain of a single discipline. It is associated with a number of disciplines - Economics, Sociology, Demography and Psychology. In developing countries like India, economic motivations influence the decisions to have large number of children. The economic value of children has two principal components: The net contribution the children make to the family's income through their labour and contribution they make later in life to the support of the aged parents, in other words, labour value of children and old age security value of children. Parents in the developing countries desire large families for good and valid economic reasons, and not because they are ignorant of how to avoid having children or acting under uncurbed passion or from blind adherence to traditional cultural norms. Where children are economically useful and cost of raising them is insignificant, it is very common for the parents to have large families. When child labour makes considerable contribution to family income and when parents are dependant on the children for protection and security in old age, there will be few incentives to reduce fertility no matter what the social cost of rapid population growth. The present book examines the economic value of children and its influence on fertility behaviour extensively.

D. Usha Rani, K. Venkatesh Babu
& M.V. Sudhakara Reddy

Introduction

Children are valuable. Fundamentally, they provide for the continuation of the human species. But this reason for wanting children is usually not uppermost in the minds of parents. To them, children are valued as sources of joy and happiness, companionship and pride. In some circumstances children may also be prized for their economic value. In this connection, *Schultz* (1974) very aptly stated that "children are a form of human Investment. The sacrifices made in bearing and rearing children are the investments. The fruits of these investments are enjoyed by the parents in the more developed countries in the form of satisfactions derived by possessing children and in less developed countries through the contribution of children to the family economy from 10 + age onwards." In other words, children have two types of utility or value to their parents non-economic and economic. At the same time, children are costly. They put added pressure on family resources, and they can in other ways curtail the activities and opportunities of parents.

These aspects of children have doubtless been evident to parents for generations. Yet it has only been recently that they have attracted scholarly attention. Demographers and others concerned with population growth and associated problems have become interested in the benefits and costs of rearing children primarily because these qualities are thought to bear an important relation to fertility behaviour. Some studies (*Mueller* 1972, *Arnold et al* 1975) have found that there is a link between attitudes towards the economic value of children and individual fertility. A number of fertility surveys (*Kuznets*, 1973; *Kasarda* 1971, *Usha Rani*, 1989) have concluded that preferences for large families are in fact linked with parents perceptions of such instrumental contributions from children as financial and practical assistance and old age support. It is argued that as economic roles for children diminish during the process of modernisation, parents perceived fewer advantages accruing from large numbers of children and consequently demand for children is correspondingly adjusted downwards. It is in this context that, off late a number of Researchers and Scholars involved in the study of population and population planning, have turned their attention to the concept of Economic value of children, i.e. the value of children as productive agents and as a source of security in old age.

Since actual decisions are taken by individual couples, the relevant question would be—what is the economic value of child at the micro level? It is true that a large component of the value of children to parents is socio-psychological in nature, and this cannot be quantified and expressed in monetary terms but it has to be admitted that, at the micro-level, economic considerations are also equally important. The available literative on the demographic transition theory, highlights the fact that in a backward agricultural economy, a child is considered to be an asset. In a developed, industrial, urban setting, however, a child becomes more of a liability than an asset. This change in the economic value of children to parents is supposed to be one of the forces that have brought about demographic transition along with the economic transformation in the western world. There is a great deal of evidence to support this view. According to *Urlanis*, the decline in the fertility rates of England and Wales in the last quarter of the 19th century was partially a function of the abolition of child labour. Recently *Kasarda* (1971) found that in the countries in which the rates of economic activity of children are low, the birthrates are significantly lower than elsewhere. An econometric analysis of the data from Puerto Rico, Egypt, Chile, Thailand and Philippines evidence of a positive relation between children's employment and the size of the family. (*Rosenzweig*, 1978) Apart from their contribution to the family income, the other economic benefits from children like help in old age, and assistance in household chores are frequently mentioned in attitudinal surveys conducted in various under developed countries. (*Betty Jamie Chung* (1972), *Mahadevan* (1987), *Bulatao* (1979). This shows that the economic value of children in developing agricultural countries is a significant factor which deserves an in-depth study.

The economic value of children in India, especially at the micro level, has been a controversial issue. Researchers (*Mamdani* (1972), *Usha Rani* (1988), *Naidu* (1983) studying this issue argued that for a majority of Indians living in rural areas, the economic value of children is positive and that this positive economic value has been a major barrier to the acceptance of family planning. Mamdani, on the basis of his study of a village in Punjab arrived at the conclusion that the only hope of a rise in status for the lower class in the village was to have a big family of sons who would either work on land for their parents and help save money or migrate to cities and send money to parents. Considering the life style of the village, he felt, that it was economically advantageous to have large families. Similar views were expressed by some other demographers. According to *Ashok Mitra* (1976), a large family is still looked upon as an asset by a vast majority of households in India. However, doubts have been expressed as to whether there is adequate actual evidence to support these observations, *Dandekar* (1977) expressed the belief that there is no adequate evidence in support of the view that the contribution of children to family income is substantial, or in support of the contention that a child is considered a benefit whose value is great but whose cost is hardly perceived at all.

Therefore, the question—what is the economic value of a child in India—remains unanswered. Unfortunately there are no comprehensive studies which can give us fairly reliable estimates of the economic value of a child in India based on systematic analysis of both benefits and costs of rearing children.

Any meaningful conclusions regarding the link between the economic value of children and fertility may be drawn only on the basis of reliable and adequate micro-level data on the actual and perceived benefits and cost of children to parents. It is obvious that such data can only be obtained through surveys—specifically designed for this purpose.

In short, in order to get a real insight into the economic value of children in India and its relation to fertility behaviour, there is a need for more comprehensive studies with the specific objective of examining the various aspects of the problem at the micro-level, namely, the actual pattern of expenditure on children, the actual economic contribution made by children, how far parents are aware of these benefits and costs, and their expectations about future benefits and costs.

In other words, the consensus arising from these diverse studies suggests that among the developing societies, the perceived and actual, current and expected contributions of children to the household economy are related with the demand for children or family size desires the extent to which these desires translate into changes in fertility behaviour both in terms of contraception and marital fertility levels is, however, not very clear. Therefore, more research not only by economists but also by sociologists and psychologists is required in order to get the real picture.

The present study is a modest attempt in this direction. The general objective of the study was to examine the relationship between the Economic value of children and Fertility Behaviour i.e. the labour value of children and old age security value of children, their determinants and relationships with fertility. Conceptually the study was based on the models of *Leibenstain* (1975) and *Hoffman and Hoffman* (1973). In addition a few other relevant models were also integrated in order to widen the scope of the study. A 'non-monetary' approach as suggested by 'Mueller' was also adopted in assessing the parental perception of benefits and costs of rearing children. As such, this work is innovative in the sense that both the actual and perceived benefits and costs of children have been examined.

The findings of the study will have several interesting policy implications. Knowledge of value of children to parents is useful for its own sake as it represents the fundamental aspect of human social behaviour. It would be helpful in understanding the determinants of human fertility. This information could be useful in making recommendations for specific social and economic policies by affecting the values of children. Further, an improved understanding of the relationship between benefits and costs of rearing children and fertility could facilitate the formulation of population policy, especially as it relates to the motives for the deterrants to fertility. It would help to anticipate ways of compensating parents of only a few children with other sources of satisfactions is the achievement of small family means couples have been deprived of some satisfactions that a large no. of children confer. Information on the Economic value of children would be especially useful in formulating alternative regarding the financial and instrumental assistance provided by children, and thus help to reduce family size preferences.

Organisation of the Thesis

The thesis was presented in eleven chapters for the sake of convenience and homogeneity in presentation of the different background and intervening variables and their influence on fertility behaviour. Although the analysis, the discussion was presented by controlling two groups namely child labour households and school children households.

In Chapter I, a comprehensive review of literature on the Economic value of children namely child labour and old age security value of children was presented. Chapter II on Methodology gives an account of the objectives, hypotheses, conceptual framework, sample frame and size, data collection, analysis and measurement of variables.

The socio-economic characteristics namely educational, occupational and economic status of the sample population were presented in the III chapter. The demographic characteristics of the sample like age at marriage and duration of marriage were discussed in the IV chapter.

The V chapter covers different dimensions of perceived economic and non-economic benefits and costs of rearing children. The relationship between child labour and fertility was examined in the VI chapter. Both the actual and perceived labour value of children were studied. Chapter VII comprehensively discussed different dimensions of old age security value of children. Value of son and fertility behaviour was dealt in the VIII chapter.

Focus of the IX chapter was on the educational and occupational aspirations for children and their effect on fertility. In the final chapter, summary of the findings, and policy implications besides some suggestion for further research were presented.

1

Review of Related Literature

In developing countries like India Economic value of children may influence to have large number of children. The value of children is a new research area, very important within the general area of fertility, particularly the micro level determinants of fertility. However, the study of economic value of children is not an exclusive domain of a single discipline. It is associated with a number of disciplines. Economics, Sociology, Demography and Psychology.

The socio-structural approach tends to be more contemporary and more action-oriented. Emphasis is given to norms, values and opportunity structures as they affect the value and cost of children for particular segments of society, especially women, and attention is directed to the need for selective purposeful, social changes to alter fertility patterns. Among the proponents of this approach are *Davis* (1967) and *Blake* (1971, 1972). A central focus of the approach is the definition of familial and non-familial roles within a society and the availability of opportunities to assume one role or another. The social structure is seen as a constraining force that operates at the individual level through the value and cost of children. As, noted by *Blake* (1972), in a very general sense, the institutional structure of every society defines and controls what is that individual couples "get out of" having children—the rewards or utilities for having a family, and how much couples must sacrifice to have them i.e. the cost. Thus, it is fair to say, that all of the specific variables that are said to "affect" family—size preferences—urbanization, educational level, possession of modern consumer goods, female labour force participation, or whatever actually may be said to effect the utility of children and their costs.

There is obviously substantial similarity between the socio-demographic and social-structural approaches. The important difference is that the social structural gives greater emphasis to mediating factors (roles, norms, the utilities and costs of children) and is oriented more toward the individual level (reproductive motivations).

The micro-economic approach, assumes that choices among competing alternatives are available and are made within a frame work of allocation of limited resources. This distinction between the micro-economic and social structural approaches led to the now-famous remark by *Duesenberry* (1960), "Economics is all about how people make choices to make". The reconciliation of these two view points has yet to occur, but it seems to be that some convergence is discernible in the area of fertility studies.

Although particular derivations of micro-economic theory tend to be complex, the underlying frame work is straight forward. A summary has been provided by *Easterlin* (1975). The conventional theory of consumer behaviour views the individual as trying to maximize satisfaction, given a range of goods, their prices, and his own tastes and income. In application of the theory of fertility analysis, children are viewed as a special kind of good, and fertility is seen as a response to the consumer's demand for children relative to other goods. In the last few years, a special variant of this approach has emerged, deriving chiefly from a 1965 article by *Becker* and distinguished by use of the concept of a "household production function".

The socio-psychological approach emphasizes the needs of individuals that are fulfilled by having children, the alternative ways of meeting those needs, and the interactions among psychological, social and economic benefits and costs of children. The socio-psychological approach tends to rely on self-reports of motivations—that is, benefits, costs and alternatives that are consciously perceived and articulated—which is both a strength and a limitation. The strength lies in the possibility of providing empirical support for certain common assumptions, such as that rural parents have a more utilitarian view of children, as well as in providing opportunities for entirely new analysis based on the patterns and strength of motivations.

The theoretical rationale for the study of value of children has been provided by *Hoffman and Hoffman* (1973). Their model contains five broad sets of variables. The value of children, alternative sources of the value, costs, barriers and facilitators. In this model, "the value of children refers to the functions the children serve or the needs they fulfil for parents". "Alternatives pertain to other avenues, besides children, for fulfilling a value. Costs refer to what must be lost or sacrificed to obtain a value in any particular way". "Barriers and facilitators refer to the factors that make it more difficult or easier to realise the particular value by having children". Further, the basic idea of the model is that fertility motivations can be analysed in terms of these five concepts".

Based on the above value scheme, the value of children project conducted in six countries (Taiwan, Korea, Philippines, Thailand, Japan and United States) on an exploratory basis developed fifteen dimensions of the perceived value of children (*Arnold, et al.*, 1975). These dimensions are as follows:

Positive values	Negative values
Emotional benefits	Emotional costs
Economic benefits and security	Economic costs
Self-enrichment and development	Restrictions or opportunity costs
Identification with children	Physical demands
Family cohesiveness and continuity.	Family costs.

Large family values	Small family values
Sibling relationships	Societal costs
Sex preference	Maternal health
Child survival	

"In this heuristic model, the dimensions of the value of children are viewed as a set of variables intervening between socio-demographic and psychological factors and social orientation on the one hand and fertility and family planning on the other (*Arnold et al* 1975).

Economic Value of Children and Fertility Behaviour

Of the various values of children, by far the most frequently studied value of children is their economic utility. In fact it is one of the few that has been directly linked to desired family size and even to contraceptive use.

According to *Ridker,* the economic value of children has two principal components: the net contribution that children make to the family's income through their work (this is, their production minus their consumption) and the contribution they make later in life to the support of aged parents.

People in different cultures and socio-economic settings want children for different reasons. *Leibenstein* (1963) identified three types of utility factors that determine the desired number of births in a family: *(a)* the utility of the child as a source of personal pleasure; *(b)* utility as a productive agent, i.e., as a source of supplementary family income and *(c)* utility as a potential source of security, either in old age or as and when necessary. The value of children symbolizes the motivations for child bearing and assumes an important role in any micro model of fertility and infra family dynamics. The value attributed to the child by the parents determine how parents behave toward the child and thus lie at the core of parent-child interaction. Cultural values seem to be quite important in determining parents expectations from children. *Hoffman and Hoffman* (1973) opined that motivation to have a child depends to a considerable extent on the value of a child to the parents.

Where children are economically useful and the cost of raising them is insignificant, it is very common for parents to have many off-spring. According to *Pearson committee.* "…. it must be recognised that in the developing world many parents want large families for good and valid economic reasons, not because they are ignorant or improvident. In such cases, access to family planning information and facilities will not make much differences. When child labour makes considerable contribution to family income, and when parents are dependent on a large family for protection and security in old age, there will be few incentives to reduce fertility no matter what the social cost of rapid population growth". (*Pearson.* 1969).

According to *Caldwell* (1982), there are two types of economics: familial-based peasant economy and non-familial based capitalist economy: these economies are distinguished by their organisation or made of production. In familial modes of production characterised by extended family obligation and assistance, the net wealth flows from younger to older generations (male) giving them decision-making power and material advantage. "Power in economic decision-making usually means power in demographic decision-making" and "High fertility is advantages to the peasant family as a whole and to its most powerful members". (*Caldwell,* 1978).

Nag et al., (1977) in their paper on "Economic value of children in two peasant societies" demonstrate that the work input by children under 15 in the Japanese and Nepalese villages in quite substantial. They also state that under the current rate of production and present circumstances, children most probably have net positive economic value for their parents in these villages, aside from the old age security provided by them. But this is contradicted by *Mueller*' (1975) who recognises children's work-input to the household productivity as a factor influencing fertility, behaviour of parents in peasant societies, but reports that data available so for has showed that "work input by child under 15 in peasant agriculture is quite limited and that children have negative economic value in peasant agriculture. *Jeejeebhoy* and *Kulkarni* (1986) opined that in a traditional society, children are perceived, on balance to be assets rather than liabilities. Therefore it is assumed that parents who expect economic assistance from children are unlikely to be sensitive to their costs.

Thus, several studies conducted in the recent period have demonstrated the potentiality of value of children in the explanation of fertility behaviour. As such, this variable is considered as not only relevant but also as important in a study of fertility behaviour.

Pro-natalist attitudes in African societies are usually expressed in the following phrase "children are better than wealth". In Nigerian segment 80 per cent of all Yoruba hold that children are either better than wealth or are wealth (*Okediji*, 1976), 78 per cent of male and 85 per cent of female respondents are of the opinion that "children are better than wealth". (*Okore*, 1977).

The International Labour Organisation (I.L.O), 1968 survey shows that high participation of children in economic activity is a common feature in developing countries. In, Sudan more than 20 per cent of the children are economically active as against 2.5 per cent in Federal Republic Germany.

According to *Paul Demeny* (1987) Children in the traditional society were on balance economically beneficial in the household: their costs were exceeded by their contribution as family labour. Economic development entailed a radical change in the balance of these components. The costs of children's upbringing soared and the economic contribution of children to the household became evanescent. In agricultural countries, virtually all members of the household except infants contributed some labour both to productive activities and to household chores. Older focus group participants confirmed that in their youth they helped their parents plant rice, take care of buffaloes, cattle, fetch water, cook food and perform other work contribute to the economic sustenance of the household (*Knodel*, 1987). Economic contributions of children influence family size preference positively at higher parities. The effect of economic contributions seem to be greatest among those with four or five or more children (*Bulato and Fawcett*, 1983).

A series of studies have examined both the economic and non-economic values of children and their links with family size desires in a number of less and more developed societies. Particularly among less developed societies, the pattern of values observed in these studies systematically support the link between the perceived economic values attached to children and family size desires.

It is clear however, that for purposes of establishing the link between the economic value of children and fertility behaviour, parent's perceptions regarding the current and expected contributions of children are of greater relevance than the actual time and labour inputs and costs of children during a fixed reference period. Such perceived values and disvalues of children as their instrumental assistance, expectations regarding old age security and sensitivity to the financial burden involved in child rearing have been analysed by value of children. Studies which examined both economic and non-economic values in diverse societies including Taiwan (*Mueller*, 1972). Thailand (*Arnold*, 1977), Gujarat and Maharashtra, (*Anker and Anker*, 1982, *Vlassoff and Vlassaff* 1980: *Kulkarni*, 1983), observed a strong positive relationship between perceived economic utility of children and fertility and a mild negative relationship between perceived costs of children and fertility. (excepting the Vlassoff study of rural Maharashtra.

In *Mueller's* (1970) study in Taiwan the parents' perception of children as economically useful was found to be related positively to the desire for a large family. The sensitivity to the expenses involved in rearing children, "costs sensitivity," on the other hand, was also measured and found to be associated with the desire for a small family. Parents who saw little utility in having large families and those who indicated cost sensitivity were also more likely to practice contraception. Further, the perceived utility of children was negatively related to the parents' education and income; and the perceived costs were positively related to education and the desire for consumer goods.

Children in the developing countries, particularly in areas where a rural economy predominates, are valued for economic reasons is well documented. The most common answers obtained in these areas to questions about why people want large families, why the respondent wants more children, and what is good about having children pertain to the economic value of children. The answers are usually phrased either in terms of the economically valuable work children perform when they are young or the old-age security they provide for the parents. In addition children may be economically valued for the "bridewealth" they bring in and also for their utility in assisting with household chores and the care of other children (*Heisel,* 1968; *Dow,* 1967; *Guthrie,* 1968; *Mysore Population Study,* 1961; *Poffenberger,* 1968; *Caldwell,* 1967; *Newton,* 1967).

The percentage of respondents who value children for economic reasons may be even higher than some of the figures indicate because other answers that are not coded as economic may nonetheless represent economic motives. For example, having many children to be sure one son will survive is often treated separately, although it may have been deprived from the need for the son to care for the parents in their old age. It is also interesting that in *Mueller's research in Taiwan* (1970), as mentioned earlier, only 12 per cent of the respondents, when asked directly to list the advantage of a large family, included the financial help they would expect to receive from the children later in life. When asked about economic expectations in old age, however, fully 73 per cent indicated that their children were to be their major source of support.

The importance of the economic value of children declines with increased industrialization and urbanization, the rise of cash in place of subsistence farming, increased pressures to send children to school, and an increase in the educational level of the parents. This pattern has been found within developing countries and in comparison between countries (*Caldwell,* 1967; *Siddiqui,* 1967; *Mueller,* 1970). It could also be noted that the same parents who stress the economic value of children are not unaware of their economic cost. For a number of reasons, however, the positive economic values may come out ahead. In many cases as often occurs in an agricultural economy, an economic need may exist for which there is no alternative but children. The nature of farming is such that there is a seasonal demand for labour rather than a steady demand. But finding workers who can be hired and fired depending on the seasons is difficult, especially when all the other industries are farms operating on the same schedule. The poor farmer cannot afford to pay for labourers, cannot live in an area where there is no income for long periods. One's own children, on the other hand, can help with farm work even when very young. Despite their cost, therefore, having children may be viewed as a necessity.

Another example of the pre-eminence of the economic value of children occurs when the economy is so close to subsistence that saving for one's old age or disability is impossible; if there is no government or private charitable institution to provide adequate care under these circumstances, then where else can one turn except to one's children? Parents and relatives of one's own age will be in the same difficult position and cannot provide help. Furthermore, in some cases, as in many parts of India, it is possible only for sons to help, since the married daughter serves her husband and his family, not her own. It is interesting to note that statistical computation by *Heer and May* (1968) indicated that in a country with a life expectancy of fifty years, five children would be necessary for a couple to be 95 per cent certain that one son would survive until the father's sixty-fifth birthday. *Poffenberger* (1968) notes that this figure seems to be the very one the Indian villagers have arrived at also, undoubtedly using more empirical than statistical procedures. Clearly from their answers the villagers are aware that to be assured of a son for old-age care, a couple must have more children than they can comfortably afford, and they usually arrive at a number between four and six. It should also be noted in passing that whereas the "ability to defer gratification" is often treated by social scientists as though it were a special quality of the wealthier classes in industrialized nations, the poor Indian villagers in Poffenberger's study are willing to undergo considerable hardship in the early years of parenthood in order to obtain that support in old age. When asked why parents would want a small family the usual response is in terms of the economic costs of children, yet these costs are tolerated for the expected later in life.

The negative value or cost of children is seen in the developing countries particularly as the areas develop the economic liabilities are increasing. The child's ability to contribute financially to the wage-earning household is limited by his skills and the child labour laws. Furthermore, the child's help is less essential; that is, the farmer's own income may depend on his children, whereas the wage earner's income, however small, is independent of the family's efforts. Pressures to send children to school often accompany modernization trends, and thus the child's help is less available even though the school schedule in rural areas is sometimes adapted to the harvest needs. Schooling also involves added costs to the parents.

Various estimates have been made of the financial expenses involved in child rearing under different economic conditions, from subsistence farming through the various economic strata in America (*Dublin and Lotka,* 1946; *Blood,* 1962; *Pohlman* 1969; *Robinson and Horlacher,* 1971). Complications and inconsistencies in these estimates arise because, apart from the actual cost of food, clothing, shelter, medical care, and education, there are different standards about what level of provision is adequate. Thus as economic well-being increases, the cost of each child increases because the standards become higher. In addition the parent's desire for competing consumer goods increases, and so also do the opportunities for the wife's employment, which become more difficult to take advantage of with additional children. Decreased-mortality effects, on the other hand, have not been considered and these would decrease financial costs; that is, in high-mortality areas parents may have to bear and care for several children for various periods in order to end up with one twelve year old. All of the estimates report that the cost of child rearing in absolute terms increases with an increased standard of living. It is also suggested, however, that as the income increases, the proportion of the total income that is spent on the child decreases. *Robinson and Horlacher* (1971) review various attempts to develop an economic theory of fertility. These use the economic theory model, but recognize the need to consider the non-monetary value of children also. Furthermore, the whole issue of alternatives to children is not handled by the approaches to date, although it is clearly essential in predicting fertility Where alternative sources of satisfaction are less, the desire for children might be greater.

Two different ways of looking at the social setting are implicit in the preceding discussion; rural versus urban and rich versus poor. The effects of urbanization are much clearer than the effects of wealth. In the rural setting as compared to the urban one the positive economic value of the child is high, the cost is low. With respect to wealth it can be said that in the absence of public provision the economic value of the child will be greater where the parents are too poor to save for old age and incapacities; and furthermore, there may be differences in the kind of economic value a child may provide (e.g., additional money versus help in the family business). But by and large there is no overwhelming effect of wealth on the child's economic contribution. On the other hand, wealth does affect the cost of the child as stated above: The absolute cost is greater among the wealthy, but the proportion of the income is less.

Similarly, *Arnold* (1975) and *Mueller* (1972) also reported that couples who want children for economic reasons tend to higher desired and actual fertility in comparison with those who want children primarily for psychological or emotional reasons.

In short, the consensus arising from these diverse studies suggests that among less developed societies, the perceived and actual, current and expected contributions of children to the household economy are positively related with demand for children or family size desires.

In this context it is important to examine the relationship between the economic value of children and fertility behaviour, particularly with reference to the developing countries like India as economic value of children is alleged to be most predominant in agricultural oriented societies.

In the following section, a comprehensive review of related studies covering the two main components of the Economic value of children i.e. child labour and old age security value of children in relation to fertility, are presented.

Child Labour and Fertility Behaviour

Labour value of children is one of the factors which motivates people, particularly in agrarian societies to have large families. *Harman* (1974) found that where opportunities exist for children to help and provide support for the family, the parents desire a larger family. Similarly *Schultz* (1974) conceived children as a form of human capital. He considers the sacrifices made in bearing and rearing children as the investments in them and the fruits of this investment are enjoyed by the parents in developing countries through the contribution of children to the family economy from 10 + age onwards. However, investment motive for wanting children can be significant only in a situation where children begin to participate to economic activities at very early ages. In most developing countries, where the cost of bearing and rearing children is low and where children enter into labour force at early ages, a surviving child seems to be a good asset. This may be the rational of rural couples preference for high fertility. There is great deal of evidence to support this contention.

A major attempt to collect valuable data on work-input of children in peasant societies was that of *Nag, White and Peet* (1978). Their study conducted in two backward communities of Java (Indonesia) and Nepal found that in both the villages economic contribution of children to the household was quite substantial. The economic contribution was measured by them in terms of the average time spent in each activity by both male and female children. In a similar study undertaken in a village—Char Gopalpur-in Bangladesh, *Cain* (1977) found that children of both the sexes put in considerably long hours of work. According to him a high fertility and a large number of surviving children are economically a rational proposition for the rural couples of Bangladesh due to their significant contribution to the household income. *Caldwell's study in Nigeria* (1977) attempted to measure and analyse the activities of children by sex, age, education and so on. Data collected by him showed that children perform variety of tasks as early as five years of age. In Philippines, *Madigan* (1977) noticed children of even less than five years of age carrying messages and making small purchases. In Thailand, *Buripkadi* (1977) observed a negative association between the expected economic help from children and both birth control attitudes of parents and the current use of birth control. He attributes this finding to the economic value attached to child labour by parents. *Peek* (1978) in an analysis of the survey data collected from two cities of the Third World tried to show to what extent the contribution of children to household income is determined by socio-economic factors. From the findings of his analysis, he concludes that the fertility levels are determined by the value of children but the economic value itself is determined by the socio-economic variables.

Similar observations, though not in detail, have been made in the Indian context. A significant one among them was that of *Mamdani* (1972). He explains why the poor households in the village Manipur desire to have large families and as such do not accept family planning. The evidence presented by him corroborates his argument that children perform variety of activities which are directly or indirectly beneficial to parents. A similar view is held by *Nadkarni* (1976). His socio-economic survey conducted on a census basis in six villages of Maharashtra State showed high child work participation rates among the small land owners and agricultural labourers. In another survey, conducted to study the economic rationality of family reproduction of a fishing community in Visakapatnam. *Murthy and Rao* (1979) observed a large proportion of children employed productively. They also observed the fertility rate of this community tending to be high.

The International Labour Organisation (I.L.O.) 1968 survey shows that high participation of children in economic activity is a common feature in developing countries. In Sudan more than 20 per cent of the children are economically active as against 2.5 per cent in Federal Republic of Germany. High fertility, high subsistence of agriculture, high economic value of children, low school enrolment and poverty are some of the contributing factors of high child labour participation in under developed countries (UDCs).

Caldwell (1977) from his research programme in Ghana, and Nigeria found that four fifths of the Youruba believe that one needs a very large number of children to ensure *(i)* that some will grow up, *(ii)* that some will be willing and able to help their parents once they are employed and *(iii)* that they will have this ability to be employed *(iv)* that some will be bright enough to win the educational qualifications that will secure them a job with a high income. There is almost unanimity in agreement about the need for this assistance in the parents old age, a view held so strong that it often obscures the profitability of such help at earlier times.

Belshaws (1956) opinion survey shows that 57 per cent of rural Japanese men expected to depend on their children in their old age as compared to 35 per cent of men in major Japanese cities and 36 per cent in smaller cities. *Lebergott* (1960) says that during the early stages of industrialization, where there is little or no compulsory education and where the laws permit child labour, children may also contributes to the family finances in the city.

Kasarda (1971) analyzes data from 49 countries correlating the per cent of population under age fifteen who were economically active in the 1960-69 period with fertility measures and finds a positive, correlation (+ 0. 54 with birth rate and 40.49 with child woman ratio, significant at .001 level). Kasarda notes that, in agricultural countries, almost six times as many females are economically active between the ages of ten and fourteen as in industrialised countries. *Vanzo* (1972) also finds a "strong positive relationship" between economic activity of children and fertility in Chile.

Mueller (1971) analysing the quality of goods consumed and work done by people at different stages of life in UDCs found that rural couples in UDCs are most worried about the cost of raising children but at the same time they also believed that their children will be an asset. In other words, they fear the financial burden of raising children, but expect in the long run to be compensated.

As is usually the case in such predicaments, one-third of all Asian children who struggle for a living do so in India—17.98 million, the largest child labour force the world has ever known. Fully 90 per cent of these children are employed in the agricultural sector, in public works such as river valley projects, in forests, fisheries and orchards—and in the cottage industries. The belief that these are harmless sectors of employment was believed as long as 1946 when the Labour Investigating committee revealed that the places of work were ill-lit, badly ventilated and that children worked as many hours as their parents. Needless to say, the committees recommendations are lying some where collecting dust in some dead file.

The general economic tables (*Census of India* 1971) reveal that the population of child workers is much higher in rural areas than in urban areas. The data shows an interesting relationship between the proportion of child workers and level of urbanization as measured by size class of towns. Higher the level of urbanization lower the percentage of economically active children. The trend is however reversed for the V and VI size class town. A plausible explanation for the inverse association between the population of child workers and level of urbanization is the higher school enrolment and fewer work opportunities for unskilled child workers in I, II, III, and IV size class towns. On the other hand, the V and VI size class towns are neither developed towns nor villages; therefore the working opportunities for children in both agriculture and industrial sectors. *Sinha* (1961) observed a similar relationship between labour force and urbanization.

Bose and Sexena (1965) in their survey in Jalore district of Rajasthan, found that of the children in the age group 10-14 years, 61 per cent are engaged in occupations, usually as family workers, the percentage of children engaged in live stock raising (grazing of sheep, goats, and cattle) is significantly greater than the percentage of adult workers. 82 per cent of the children are engaged in cultivation, 12 per cent in live stock raising, 4 per cent in agricultural and causal labour and 2.2 per cent in other occupations.

An excellent sample survey of 211 working children by *Singh, Kama and Khan* of the National Institute of Public Cooperation and Child Development, New Delhi (1979) revealed that 54 were employed in production units, 47 in repair and services, 45 in domestic work, 21 in construction work, 17 in sales and vending, 15 in arts and crafts and 8 in hotels.

The problem of child labour in India is enormous in its magnitude. "To begin with, India has no consensus-based chronological definition of child labour". For, although article 24 of the Indian Constitution lays down that "No child below the age of 14 shall be employed in work in any factory or mine or be engaged in any hazardous occupation", the age limit differs from 12 to 14 with each of the 13 different legislations pertaining to children. The loopholes in the law are also numerous. The Employment of Children's Act, 1938, for example, states that "No child who has not completed 15 years shall be employed or permitted to work in any occupation connected with the transport of passengers, goods or mail by railway or a port authority within the limits of the port". As a result, many kinds are forced to seek employment in the unorganised sector where they are worse off, since employment in the unorganised sector where they are worse off, since employment conditions cannot be regulated. Yet, in cases where labour inspectors do come across child workers, they turn a blind eye. Says Mr. *Bhave*: the Labour Commissioner of Bombay "when the employer explains that he took in a child out of pity for his starving condition or that the child is an orphan, my men let him pass out of compassion". Inspectors are also aware that as soon as they enter a factory, children who are obviously under-age are made to escape through the backdoor. Those who can't are tutored to give up work for the duration of the inspection while the employer explains that the child has brought in someone's tiffin, a message from home or has been brought to the work-place as there is no one to care for him at home. Children are also not entered into any register where they can be checked out. "With no record of their employment and with their active connivance, it is very difficult to prove that certain organisations abuse child workers".

Therefore given analysis not only reveals a strong positive relationship between child labour force and family size desires, but also the numerous dimensions of the problems of child labour with demographic, social and economic implication. Generally in agricultural communities the thinking is that, more number of children in the family would fetch more income for the family. But, actually speaking child labour deprives children of educational opportunities, minimises their chances for vocational training, stunts their physical growth, hampers their intellectual development and forces them to remain as unskilled labourers with low wages all their lives. A similar trend was found by *Pant* (1965). More over, child labour affects adversely the employment opportunities for adults. *Chandra* (1961) estimates that if all the children were eliminated from the labour forces of India, employment opportunities would be created for at least 15 million adult unemployed workers and thereby lessen the problem of unemployment in the country to a very great extent. However, research on the relative merits of various policy alternatives for removing children from the labour force is very limited. Analysing United Area Republic Census Data, *Schultz* and

Vanzo (1970) estimated that a decrease in the proportion of unpaid family workers in labour force brought about through advances in women's intermediate education, world be associated with a decline in surviving fertility between 7 and 9 per cent. However the real extent to which compulsory schooling would be effective is not clear for even with 5 to 6 hours in school, education can still contribute to family income (occanional Monograph Series No. 2 ICP). Different improvements in agricultural technology could alternatively 'free' children by decreasing the relatives value of their labour or encourage increased population by decreasing the value of their labour. Therefore, immediate research on ways and means to effectively eliminate child labour from the over all labour force is essential.

To conclude, one can state that the problem of child labour is multidimensional which needs multi-pronged attack. However, as long as the Indian economy remains predominantly agricultural, where more than 70 per cent of the population subsist on it, it may not be easy to solve the problem of child labour. In fact, here children are considered poorman's capital. To most of the Indians, the value contributed by the labour of their children is far more greater than the cost of feeding them (*Social Scientist,* 1974).

However, there are very few studies directly focussing on child labour and its dimensions. The need for primary data investigating the causes and consequences of child labour is deeply felt especially in the Indian context. To solve this problem of child labour, it is essential to study it is different groups with varying backgrounds. Detailed information on the asset ownership educational, occupational and economic statuses of the parents of child labour etc. would be very useful in identifying the various factors leading to high child-work participation rates.

OLD AGE SECURITY VALUE OF CHILDREN AND FERTILITY BEHAVIOUR

Children are economically valued not only for labour or income but also for old age security to the parents. People in the developing countries are often heard to say that 'children are the security of parents in old age. Most of the parents expect their children to provide for them in their old age. The more children they have, the more assured they are of economic support, physical care and attention when they are old and can no longer earn and take care of themselves. Consequently children are never looked upon as a financial burden. Also may parents seldom consider the fact that children have to be fed, clothed, sheltered, educated and provided with other needs upto 10 to 15 years or so before they can be become economically productive. Further, parents rarely take into account the fact that opportunities of children to get higher education and thereby improve their earning capacity become limited as the number of children in the family increases, given the limited income of the family.

Numerous attitudinal surveys have revealed that children are important for providing old age security to parents. In Nigeria, as high as 95 per cent of the parents felt that: "Children are important because of the help they give to parents when they are old" (*Caldwell,* 1976). The value of Children Project has shown that in all countries more than 70 per cent of rural respondents expect to rely on their children when they are old (*Arnold et al.,* 1975). In Thailand, data on expected living arrangements of parents in old age reveal that 84 per cent of the respondents expected to live with children in their old age *(Arnold and Pejaranonda,* 1977). An analysis of the residential pattern of elderly persons in the Nepalese village shows that people depend more on their sons than their daughters for old age security. In the Javanese village, however, the parents are almost equally dependent on sons and daughters in their old age. This is attributed to the somewhat flexible pattern of marital residence in Java (*Nag et al.,* 1978).

The striking Japanese experience was reported by *Freedman* (1968) as an illustration of the relation between old age dependence norm and fertility. In Japan's Case, *Kobayashi* (1977) found that "an almost simultaneous and parallel start of a change can be seen in the limitation of fertility and .... the feeling of dependence on children in old age". With Taiwanese data, *Harmalin* (1976)—finds a fairly strong relation between ideal number of children and the level of assistance expected from married sons. *Neher* (1971) believed that population size can be significantly reduced if alternative pension schemes are made available. Similarly, *Hohm* (1975) has shown that social security programmes have had a negative effect on subsequent levels of fertility in a large number of countries.

Children are considered as attractive investments, because "a child draws upon resources when they are relatively plentiful and provides a return source of support in old age" (*Schultz*, 1971). In a different context *Caldwell* (1976) emphasizes: "Investment in children is probably an investment in the real sense of the term". Educated children when they are employed in modern sector and have reached their occupational heights, 'they will, in most cases, return more money and remit it more regularly".

Favouring child investments, *DeTray* (1976) argues that the capital markets in developing countries are imperfect and in comparison with alternative investments child investments yield the least negative return. On the contrary, both *Robinson* (1972) and *Ohlin* (1971) believe that children are not a good investment for old age. Further, *Mueller* (1976) points out that in low-income countries "older rural males continue to work on the family farm and thus may require little old age support from their children". *Repetto* (1976) argues that the capital markets do exist and substantial transactions are taking place in rural areas of low-income countries. But all such arguments may not deny the fact that in developing countries a high proportion of older women are widows and their economic security primarily lies in their sons (*Ridker*, 1976). Likewise, older persons may do little "economic work" that justifies their economic self-reliance. Moreover, not only monetary support, but other forms of physical and emotional supports deserve equal attention for the proper evaluation of old age security investments on children. Perhaps, in developing countries, no investment is as attractive as a child until a considerable level of institutional sophistication has been achieved (*Ware*, 1978).

In countries like India that do not have a well-developed system of pensions, social security, unemployment compensation, and other insurance schemes, children particularly sons are the only reliable source of security for their parents in old age. This "pension motive" is rather forcible in traditional societies characterized by strong family Kinship ties (*Mueller*, 1972; *Chung*, 1972; *Repetto*, 1976). The available evidence in India on the pronatalist effect of old age support motive is mostly qualitative and indirect (*Poffenberger and Poffenberger*, 1973; *U.N.*, 1961; *Mandelbaum*, 1974; *Khan*, 1977). From these studies it appears that son preference is synonymous with old age security motive. An All India Sample Survey conducted in 1970 has shown that 56 per cent of the couples desire a son "to support the family" (*ORG*, 1973). *Mamdani* (1972) maintains that "Since daughters must always marry outside the village, security for old age depends solely on the number of sons a couple has".

Mukherjee (1973) notes that "the Indian people, on an average, desire two sons: one, at the minimum, to look after them in their old age since most of them have hardly any savings to fall back upon, and the second as an insurance against death or any calamity befalling the other". Some have attempted to calculate the number of sons required to ensure the survival of at latest one son in order to provide support to the parents in old age (*May and Heer*, 1968; *Heer and Smith*, 1967; *Ridker*, 1969). They have shown that in countries like India with 50 years of life expectancy a couple must bear five children to ensure with 95 per cent confidence the survival of at least one son on the father's sixty-fifth birthday (*Poffenberger*, 1968; *Poffenberger* and *Poffenberger*, 1973; *Mandelbaum*, 1974).

Though all these studies state the importance of old age security value of children in India, very few studies have attempted to study the strength of old age security motive in influencing fertility behaviour. However, *Mahadevan* (1979) who has studied a number of roles of children in relation to fertility concludes: 'compared to the other roles, old age support is considered to be the most common role'. Further an overwhelming majority of the respondents favour sons as old age security providers as against daughters. It is also found that the importance attached to this role is associated with higher fertility particularly in the lower caste groups.

Against this picture, some are sceptical about the direct linkage between old age security motive and reproductive behaviour as the latter precedes much earlier than the former (*Dandekar,* 1975; *Vlassoff and Vlassoff,* 1980). Based on a study in rural Maharashtra, *Vlassoff and Vlassoff* (1980) have concluded that "economic resources, not an abundance of sons, are relevant factors that determine security in old age". However, much credence need out be accorded to this finding as the economic status is not controlled in the analysis. Moreover, the same study revealed that for more than 90 per cent of the widowed, separated and aged-respondents sons are a major source of old age security. This is true particularly in the case of Indian widows. According to 1971 census, more than 60 per cent of the women in the age group 60-64 were widowed. For these women, security lies principally in their sons, but not in daughters or sons-in-law for many reasons (*Poffenberger,* 1968; *Poffenberger* and *Poffenberger,* 1973; *Mandelbaum,* 1974).

However, old age security value of children, inspite of being a crucial determinant of fertility behaviour in most developing countries, still remains the least analyzed variable. There is widespread disagreement on its importance in developing countries. *Leibenstein* (1957, 1975) and others argue that it is the most important motive while *Lindert* (1980, 1983) and others consider its influence on fertility as negligible. Under these circumstances, the dearth of adequate empirical analyses on the subject is a serious shortcoming (*Stolnitz,* 1983). The present study is an attempt in this direction.

From the review of literature on the Economic value of Children and fertility, it may be seen that benefits and costs of children, labour value of children and old age security have a bearing of fertility bahaviour of couples. Presently, there is awareness among individuals all over the world regarding the costs and benefits involved in having children, to some degree of other. In India, too, the intensity of this consciousness is slowly gaining ground. However, to encourage this rational reasoning and break up from traditional beliefs, there is need for information regarding the various components of the Economic value of children, thus necessitating primary investigation, the present study was taken up with the objective of collecting detailed information on the two components of Economic value of children—child labour and old age security.

2

Methodology

'The Value of Children' is a concept that has been given some attention by demographers, economists, psychologists and anthropologists. In general, this attention has been at a theoretical or conceptual level, little empirical research has been done. This area of research closely related to fertility has been curiously neglected. Research on this topic has important implications for population policies which can use data on benefits and costs as guidance for policies that would provide alternative sources of satisfaction or policies that would increase the actual or perceived costs of children; family planning communication programmes many make use of this data as audience research on motivations for parenthood; and understanding and prediction of fertility behaviour. For these purposes, among others, a substantial effort to investigate the values of children is clearly essential, especially as it has great potentiality for policy formulation and programme development in the field of fertility control. Such policies and programmes are useful to countries that wish to accelerate fertility declines.

Of the various values of rearing children, 'The economic value of children' is alleged to be the most predominant factor in influencing fertility behaviour particularly in agrarian societies. A comprehensive review of related literature (vide chapter I) showed that very few studies have directly focussed on the relationship between economic value of children and fertility behaviour. As such, the present study was undertaken in an attempt to asses this relationship.

Objectives

The general objective of the study was to compare the effect of Economic Value of children on Fertility behaviour across two broad sectors—Child Labour Households (CLH) and School Going Children Households (SGCH). Relationship of other conventional socio-economic and demographic variables with fertility was also examined. The specific objectives of the study were:

1. To collect detailed demographic and socio-economic information from the respondents with special reference to economic values of children and fertility behaviour;
2. To expand our knowledge on the subject of economic value of children as a motive for high fertility;
3. To collect data on the perceived benefits and costs of rearing children across the two sectors and examine their relationship with differential fertility;
4. To compare fertility levels and differential in the child labour and school going children households;
5. To identify micro determinants of child labour participation;
6. To asses sectoral differences in the perceived labour value of children and its impact on fertility behaviour;
7. To analyse and compare the expectations of child labour and school going children households regarding old age support;
8. To study the degree of son preference prevalent among the two sector—CLH and SGCH;
9. To investigate the differences in parental aspirations for children and its influence on fertility;
10. To examine the living conditions of the two sectors—CLH and SGCH;

11. To study other related socio-economic and demographic variables and their relationship with fertility.
12. To study the family size preferences of the child labour and child schooling sectors.
13. To know the attitude of the CLH and SGCH towards family planning.

Hypotheses

Based on the above objectives, the following hypotheses were framed for testing:

1. Differences in perceived benefits and costs of rearing children influence fertility behaviour differentially among the child labour and school going children households;
2. The Economic Value of Children will be higher among the child labour households than the school going children households;
3. Perceived benefits of rearing children are directly and perceived costs of rearing children and inversely related to fertility;
4. Higher the economic value of children, higher the fertility;
5. Higher the perception about children's willingness to help parents in old age, higher the fertility;
6. Preference for Son will be greater among the CLH than the SGCH;
7. The pattern of living arrangements differs between the SGCH and CLH;
8. Socio-economic status of SGCH would be higher than that of CLH;
9. Higher socio-economic status effectively depresses fertility levels irrespective of other factors;
10. Age at marriage is inversely related to fertility and duration of marriage directly;

11. Preferred ideal family size will be larger among the CLH than the SGCH;
12. Attitude towards family planning will be more favourable among the SGCH compared to CLH;
13. The SGCH will have higher educational and occupational aspirations than the CLH the study was carried out controlling the two sectors—child labour households and school going children households, since values of rearing children are likely to vary among different strata of the rural population.

Conceptual Framework

The conceptual Models of Leibenstein (1975) and *Hoffman and Hoffman* (1986) formed the overall basis for the present research. A few other relevant models (*Easterlin,* 1975; *Mueller,* 1975; Value of children project by *Arnold et al.,* 1975) were also adapted as per the requirements of the study. For operational convenience, a simplified version of all the above models was formulated. In this tentative model, child labour and child schooling are viewed as key variables, intervening between socio-economic and demographic factors on the one hand and fertility on the other. It is further, assumed that child labour, child schooling old age security and values of children are all interrelated despite their individual effect on fertility. While the first three variables represent the actual status of children, the latter denotes the perceived status of children. Equal empahsis is placed on both the aspects in explaining fertility differentials.

Sample Frame and Size

(a) . Study Area

The study was carried out in the rural areas of Chittoor district i.e. Srikalahasthi, Puttur and Chandragiri Mandals. Chittoor of the quartlets of Rayalaseema was purposively selected as this district had characteristics more or less similar to other districts in Andhra Pradesh. Chittoor is the Southern most district of A.P. sharing its borders with the states of Tamil Nadu and

Karnataka. According to 1981 census Chittoor ranks 7th in area and 5th in population in A.P. of the form districts of Rayalaseema, Chittoor is the most densely populated (181 persons per Sq. km.), highest literate (31.6%) and the least urbanished (5%). Another important characteristic of this district is that it is prove to recurring droughts.

Chittoor is predominantly an agrarian district. Of the total workers, 80.4 per cent are employed in primary, 7.2 per cent in secondary and 12.4 per cent in tertiary sectors. Srikalahasthi, Puttur and Chandragiri Mandals were selected for the present study as child labour, the group to be studied were distributed in sizable proportions in these Mandals. In these Mandals, child labour participation in Beedi-making factory, glass-heads factory, Handloom weaving, Basket-making and agricultural operations was very high. Both boys and girls were employed with substantial wages.

(b) Respondents

The respondents of the study represented one broad section of the population i.e. Non-Scheduled Caste (NSC) the respondents belonged to the NSC population namely Reddy, Kamma, Balja and Naidu. Who by and large have similar socio-cultural backgrounds. The NSCs occupy the upper stratum of the social hierarchy. A significant proportion of them are agriculturists, tenants and agricultural labourers. Excessive dependence on monsoon has resulted in constant fluctuations in their fortunes leading to economic insecurity. Off late, some youngsters have been taking advantage of the self-employment schemes and have started cottage industries like poultries, Dairy-farms, Handloom weaving etc. the NSCs, in a lid to maintain prestige spend a great deal of their income of social functions like marriages, festivals, death and birth ceremonies. In view of their similar characteristics, a few relatively homogenous castes have been grouped together under the category of Non-Scheduled Castes.

(c) Sampling

The respondents of the study were chosen from the rural areas of Chittoor district of Andhra Pradesh, India. The sampling unit for the study was an eligible couple in the reproductive age span of 15-44 years, with two or more living children and the last child they posses in the age group of 9-14 years. A list of eligible couples in the sample areas, satisfying the sample criteria was prepared for both the child labour households and school going children households separately. Using stratified random sampling technique, a sample of 150 was selected from each list, representing households from both the sectors—CLH and SGCH. An equal sample was preferred to facilitate comparison between the two sectors. Further, it would help to match the sample in the two sectors with regard to all traits.

Conceptual Frame Work

Socio-economic and Demographic factors	Values of children
Caste, age, sex,	Child labour and child schooling
Education,	Old age security Value of children
Occupation	
Income	Son preference
Health, age at marriage	
Duration of marriage	Benefits and costs of rearing children.

Family size preferences

Contracepture Behaviour

Thus the total sample consisted of 300 households, comprising 150 child labour households and 150 school going children households.

The sample for each village was computed using the formula:

$$ni = \frac{Ni}{Ni} . n$$

Where Ni = Number of eligible couples in the village

Ni = Total number of eligible couples in the universe

n = Sample size (150)

In the case of households having more than one eligible couple, only one couple was chosen randomly, as most of the background characteristics would be the same.

Sample size
(N = 300)

Child labour households	School going children households
(N = 150)	(N = 150)

Data Collection

(a) Interview Schedule

Data for the present study was collected through personal interviewing of all the cases with a schedule. The interview technique was used as the basic method of data collection as the sample included many respondents with little or no education. In addition it was recognized that the study could not be conducted through a simple 'opinion' survey. Thus a schedule incorporating all the measures of Economic Value of children was prepared and personally filled up by the investigator. The schedule consisted of a no. of sections covering household particulars, personal information, Socio-economic variables, Demographic variables, Benefits and costs of rearing children, Child labour, old age security value of children, value of son, educational and occupational aspirations for children, family size preferences and contraceptive behaviour. To improve the quality of the data, a short term participant observation was also adopted while collecting data.

(b) Interview Process

Before starting the actual collection of data, the investigator visited the sample area and established support with the sample population—Prominent people in the village such as village health worker, School teacher, Doctor, Village President etc. who ever available was approached to introduce the investigator to the respondents. Appointments were fixed with them giving priority to their convenience and leisure. This helped the investigator to collect even delicate personal information.

OPERATIONAL DEFINITIONS

Child Labour Household (CLH)

1. A household with at least one child in the age group of 9-14 years and employed in the labour force for wages is defined as child labour household.
2. School Going Children Household (SGCH)

A household with at least on child in the age group of 9-14 years and all the children attending school regularly is defined as school going children household.

MEASUREMENT OF VARIABLES

Value of Children

The perception on costs and benefits of rearing children were broadly grouped into four categories, i.e. economic costs, non-economic costs, economic benefits and non-economic benefits.

The economic costs include perception of parents towards children as a financial burden, savings for children's future education, marriages, costs of child rearing precluding over all other purchases, pre-occupation with child rearing as a cause for not working now and higher child costs as a cause for taking up employment.

The perceived non-economic costs were like noise and disorder in the house, extra house work, general wariness to the mother, lack of time, sleep and worry to the parents and such other costs i.e., adverse effects of large number of children (4+) on the well being of a household.

Perceived economic benefits from children were the parents perception of instrumental assistance and old age security benefits from children. Instrumental assistance refers to help on the farm, business, house work and the child's contribution to the families finances. Perception of old age security consists of the extent to which parents expect to receive in the form of financial support and residence with their children, especially sons in their old age.

Perceived non-economic benefits from children consisted of costs incurred by the parents as a source of joy and happiness, as a bond between husband and wife, for fulfillment of marriage, to attain adult status and social prestige, continuity of family name and tradition, producing heirs and performing of funerals.

It is difficult to measure and interpret variables based on individual perceptions. In order to enhance the explanatory power of attitudinal variables (costs and benefits), a better methodological approach using an index combining all the specific attitudinal statements was adopted. This was considered a better methodological approach as measurement was bound to improve when answers to several related questions are taken into account. Further the analysis is much easier to carry out, when the number of variables is reduced by combining them into indices.

To measure the perceived costs and benefits of rearing children, an index was constructed based on the scaled response to attitude—statement reflecting each dimensions of the costs and benefits of children. Each response of the attitude scale on perceived benefits and costs of rearing children was assigned a score value—3 for 'agreement', 2 for 'uncertainty' and 1 for 'disagreement'. Scoring pattern and scaled response dimension used in the index construction for cumulative perceived economic and non-economic costs and economic and non-economic benefits of rearing children was derived from total sum of scores assigned to the respective costs and benefits of rearing children.

Index	Score range
Low (disagree)	10-16
Medium (uncertainty)	17-23
High (agree)	24-30

Parental Perception on Old Age Security

The combined effect of variables on parental perception such as, children's willingness to live with their parents after the marriage, supporting their aged parents, helping in household maintenance, providing adequate recreation and entertainment, sharing personal responsibilities (apart from financial help) etc., was examined by developing an index. Based on the cumulative score of the individual on these variables, the respondents were classified into two categories. This procedure helped to make wider generalisation.

Index	Score range
Low (less willing)	10-15
High (more willing)	16-20

Fertility Variables

Total number of live births is the major fertility variable (dependent variable) considered in this analysis. All the tabulations were carried out for this variable only. However, family size norms—additional expected and ideal family size norms—were also presented as fertility indices to supplement live births for predicting the future fertility behaviour.

3

Socio-economic Characteristics and Fertility Behaviour

The historical experience of the developed countries and findings from a number of studies (*U.N.*, 1965; *Freedman*, 1959; *Johnson*, 1967; *Kiser et al.*, 1968) have highlighted that there was a general coherence between socio-economic development and demographic change. Today it is widely recognized that the real motivation for a small family springs from various aspects of economic and social development. As such the complex inter relationship between fertility and socio-economic factors has been receiving growing attention from researchers, planners and administrators. However, a major problem faced by them is the lack of data that adequately reflects these relationships in different population groups. Therefore, realising that one of the unique features of a fertility study is the possibility it offers to relate socio-economic characteristics to reproductive behaviour, the present chapter examined the socio-economic characteristics of the respondents in relation to their fertility behaviour.

Education and Fertility

Toady, there is widespread contention that spread of education is necessary for effective implication of Health and

Family welfare programmes, as illiterate people find it difficult to comprehend new ideas such as birth control and contraceptives. Education would go a long way in making new ideas acceptable to people. A number of studies have bound that education and fertility are inversely related. (*Nerlove and Schultz,* 1970; *Usha Rani,* 1989; *Miro and Mertens,* 1968; *Bhende and Rao,* 1969; *Registrar General of India,* 1972). The present data also confirmed the hypothesis that education has a very strong inverse relationship with fertility.

Table—3.1. Percentage Distribution of School Going Children Households (SGCH) and Child Labour Households (CLH) by Educational Status and Mean Live Births.

Educational Status	SGCH		CLH	
	%	**MLB**	**%**	**MLB**
Illiterates	16.00 (24)	3.83 (24)	52.00 (78)	4.12 (78)
Primary	26.00 (39)	3.23 (39)	22.67 (34)	3.80 (34)
Secondary	35.33 (53)	2.84 (53)	18.66 (28)	3.42 (28)
College level	22.67 (34)	2.44 (34)	6.67 (10)	2.90 (10)
Total	**100.00** **(150)**		**100.00** **(150)**	

Significant differences existed between SGCH and CLH with respect to their educational status. A large percentage of the SGCH had higher educational levels. Only one fourth of the CLH had secondary and college level education as against more than half of the SGCH. Among the CLH there were 52 per cent illiterates to 16 per cent of the SGCH 84 per cent of the SGCH were educated while in contrast only less than 50 per cent of the CLH respondents had education.

The data showed inverse relationship existed between the education level of the respondents and their fertility behaviour thus confirming the hypothesis that higher the educational level, lower the fertility. Both among the SGCH and CLH, fertility declined consistently with increasing educational levels. However SGCHs had lower fertility compared to SLHs.

Among SGCH, those with college education had 0.40 MLB less than the respondents who had secondary education as against their counterparts who had 0.52 less MLB among the CLH.

Those who had no education, had 0.50 more MLB among the SCH's and 0.32 more MLB among the CLH's as compared to the respondents who had primary education. This clearly reveals the impact of education on fertility. The data highlights the decisive influence of education in depressing fertility.

Occupation

Occupation of the husband, has probably been the most utilized index of socio-economic status in the study of fertility differentials changes in occupational distribution of the population of industrially advanced countries have accompanied the general declines in fertility. Relatively high fertility has been associated with the primary industries, particularly agriculture and mining, while lower rates of fertility have been associated with the professional classes, white collar workers and urban industrial workers.

Significant occupational differences existed among the two groups. The SGCH had comparatively higher occupational status with nearly fifty per cent of them being employees. More than a quarter of them were engaged in miscellaneous activities with a small percentage in cultivation. Less than 10 per cent of the SGCH were daily workers. In contrast, one third of the CLH were cultivators, while another one third were daily workers. 27 per cent of the CLH were also engaged in miscellaneous activities like small business, vendors etc.

Table—3.2. Percentage Distribution of the School Going Children Households and Child Labour Households by Occupational Status and Mean Live Births.

Occupational Status	SGCH %	SGCH MLB	CLH %	CLH MLB
Employees	49.33 (74)	2.62 (74)	5.33 (8)	2.87 (8)
Cultivators	13.33 (20)	3.25 (20)	34.67 (52)	3.58 (52)
Daily workers	9.34 (14)	3.85 (14)	32.67 (49)	3.97 (49)
Others (petty business, vendors, etc.)	28.00 (42)	3.71 (42)	27.33 (41)	4.16 (41)
Total	**100.00 (150)**	**3.01 (150)**	**100.00 (150)**	**3.84 (150)**

The data confirmed the hypothesis that occupational status differentially influences fertility behaviour. In both the groups, respondents with higher occupational status had lower fertility. In both the SCH and CLH groups, employees had lowest fertility (2.62 MLB for the SCH and 2.87 MLB of the CLH). Daily workers and those engaged in miscellaneous activities had relatively higher fertility of 3.85 MLB and 3.71 MLB in the SCH groups and 3.97 MLB and 4.16 MLB in the CLH groups respectively, with the cultivators ranging in between. In all occupations, CLH respondents had higher fertility. The high fertility of the CLHs may be due to the fact that low income earners who constitute this category normally go for more children than the desired number, for various reasons, such as the poor security, low economic status, traditional ways of living etc. The actual and perceived economic value of children for the CLH groups seems to be very high. The data also confirmed the contention that generally people engaged in traditional occupations perceived— high economic benefits from children and prefer to have large families relative to those engaged in modern and non-agricultural occupations.

EXPENDITURE AND FERTILITY BEHAVIOUR

Economic status of the individual has a major influence on the fertility behaviour. The expenditure of the individual on his family is also an indicator of his economic status. Generally better standards of living and higher economic status have declining influence on fertility. Indian data shows that where monthly expenditure is high, fertility is low. In sample survey conducted by *Registrar General's Office* (1972), it was found that as consumption expenditure increased, fertility decreased sharply. Thus, an attempt was made to examine the relationships between expenditure and fertility.

Table—3.3. Percentage Distribution of School Going Children Households and Child Labour Households by Annual Expenditure and Mean Live Birth.

Expenditure in Rs.	SGCH		CLH	
	%	MLB	%	MLB
Below 6000	13.33 (20)	3.60 (20)	42.00 (63)	4.06 (63)
6001-12000	21.33 (32)	3.06 (32)	32.00 (48)	3.87 (48)
12001 and above	65.34 (98)	2.87 (98)	26.00 (39)	3.45 (39)
Total	**100.00 (150)**	**3.01 (150)**	**100.00 (150)**	**3.84 (150)**

The data revealed that significant variations existed between SGCH and CLH with regard to their annual expenditure. In the sample area, more than three-fifths of SGCH respondents (65.34%) were spending Rs. 12001/- and above per annum for family expenditure as against one quarter in the case of CLHs. As indicated by their low occupational status, 42 per cent of the CLHs were spending less than Rs. 6000/- per annum for their family maintenance as against only 13 per cent of the SGCH families.

The data revealed that an inverse relationship between the respondents expenditure on family maintenance and their level of fertility. Both among SCH and CLH with increase in the family expenditure, a significant decline in their fertility may be observed.

INCOME AND FERTILITY

Income is one of the most important variables which influenced the fertility behaviour of an individual. Many studies have found an inverse relation between economic status as measured by income and fertility. (*Rain Water,* 1965; *Freedman* et al, 1959; U.N. 1973; *Saxsena,* 1973; *Usha Rani,* 1989) It has been contended that with increasing income basic necessities of life are satisfied and rational planning for one's future and that of one's children becomes possible and increasing wealth might thus lead to decrease in fertility.

It is very difficult to estimate and collect information on income as most people either withhold or do not give correct information relating to their assets for a number of reasons such as fear of imposition of income tax, loss of subsidies and benefits the Government has provided for economically backward classes. However, keeping in view the paucity of data on income, an attempt has been made to examine this variable as well as its relationship with fertility.

The respondents were divided into four groups based on their annual income. The data revealed that SGCH and CLH differed significantly from each other with respect to their annual income. Among the SGCH only 13 per cent of them had an annual income below Rs. 5000/- and one fifth had 5001 to 15000 and about one third (34%) had an income of above Rs, 25,000/– on the other hand 40 per cent of the CLH had an income below Rs. 5000/- and only one fifth had income above Rs. 25,000/-. It is clear that the CLH had a lower economic status as against the SGCH.

Table—3.4. Percentage Distribution of School Going Children Households and Child Labour Households by Income and Mean Live Birth.

Income levels	SGCH		CLH	
	%	MLB	%	MLB
Below 5000	13.33 (20)	3.70 (20)	42.00 (63)	4.17 (63)
5001-15000	21.33 (32)	3.37 (32)	28.00 (42)	3.91 (42)
15001-25000	31.34 (47)	3.06 (47)	17.33 (26)	3.76 (26)
25001 +	34.00 (51)	2.59 (51)	12.67 (19)	2.68 (19)
Total	**100.00 (150)**	**3.01 (150)**	**100.00 (150)**	**3.84 (150)**

A strong inverse relationship may be observed between the income level of the respondents and their fertility. It is clearly evident from the data that with increase in the household income, fertility declined consistently. This trend may be noted in the case of both school going children households and child labour households. The high income group had the lowest fertility both among SGCH and CLH (2.5 and 2.6 MLB respectively) and the low income group had the highest fertility. (3.7 and 4.1 MLB respectively) Even the lower and higher income groups had lower fertility than the low income group.

The data suggests that economic status of the respondents is a major factor in determining family size of the respondents.

Socio-economic Status and Fertility

A number of studies (*Reddy*, 1986; *Kocher*, 1976; *Rele and Kanitker*, 1980) conducted in India and elsewhere have confirmed that socio-economic status is inversely related to fertility.

Differential fertility by socio-economic status appears to be more striking than each socio-economic variable independently. As such, in order to examine the combined influence of all the socio-economic variable together on fertility, an index was constructed.

Table—3.5. Percentage Distribution of School Going Children Households and Child Labour Households by Socio-Economic Status Index and Mean Live Birth.

Socio-economic status Index	SGCH		CLH	
	%	MLB	%	MLB
Low SES	33.33 (50)	3.52 (50)	71.33 (107)	4.87 (107)
Middle SES	40.00 (60)	3.01 (60)	22.00 (33)	3.75 (33)
High SES	26.67 (40)	2.50 (40)	6.67 (10)	2.90 (10)
Total	**100.00** **(150)**	**3.01** **(150)**	**100.00** **(150)**	**3.84** **(150)**

The respondents were stratified into three broad socio-economic status levels—Low, Middle and High socio-economic status. Significant differences existed between the respondents of the two sectors in relation to their socio-economic status. (More than one-fourth (27%) of the respondents in SGCHs had high socio-economic status, relative to only 7 per cent in the CLHs). The percentage of respondents in the SGCH (40%) who had medium socio-economic status was double that of those in the CLHs (22%). In contrast, more than double the number of CLHs had lower socio-economic status (71%) as compared to the SGCHs (33%).

In both the sectors, a clear trend of strong inverse relationship between socio-economic status and fertility, confirmed the hypothesis that couples with help socio-economic status had lower fertility and vice-versa. (In the SGCH and CLH, the respondents with higher socio-economic status had 2.50 and 2.90 MLB as against 3.52 and 4.87 MLB for those with low socio-economic status). The fertility of the respondents with medium socio-economic status was also less. (3.01 and 3.75 MLB). The data indicated that socio-economic status had strong influence of fertility.

Sum Up

Significant differences existed between SGCH and CLH with respect to their education status. A large percentage of the SGCH had higher educational levels. Only one fourth of CLH had secondary and college level education as against more than half of the SGCH. Among the CLH there were 52 per cent illiterates to 16 per cent of the SGCH. The data showed inverse relationship existed between the education level of the respondents and their fertility. Both among the SGCH and CLH, fertility declined consistently with increasing educational levels. However, SGCHs had lower fertility compared to CLHs. Occupational differences existed among the two groups. The SGCH had comparatively higher occupational status with nearly fifty per cent of them being employees. Less than 10 per cent of the SGCH were daily workers. In contrast, one third of the CLH were cultivators, while another one third were daily workers. In both the groups, respondents with higher occupational status had lower fertility. In both the SGCH and CLH groups, employees had lowest fertility (2.62 MLB for the SGCH and 2.87 MLB of the CLH). Daily workers and those engaged in miscellaneous activities had relatively higher fertility of 3.85 MLB and 3.71 MLB in the SGCH groups and 3.97 MLB and 4.16 MLB in the CLH groups respectively, with the cultivators ranging in between.

Significant variations existed between SGCH and CLHs with regard to their annual expenditure. In the sample area, more than three-fifths of SGCH respondents (65.34%) were spending Rs. 12001/- and above per annum for family expenditure as against one quarter in the case of CLHs. Both among SGCH and CLH with increase in the family expenditure, a significant decline in their fertility may be observed. SGCH and CLH differed significantly from each other with respect to their annual income. Among the SGCH only 13 per cent of them had an annual income below Rs. 5000/- and one fifth had 5001 to 15,000 and about one third (34%) had an income of above Rs. 25, 000/- on the other hand 40 per cent of the CLH had an income below Rs. 5,000 and only one fifth had income above Rs. 25,000/-. The high income group had the lowest fertility both among SGCH and CLH (2.5 and 2.6 MLB respectively) and the low income group had the highest fertility. More than one-fourth (27%) of the respondents in SGCHs had high socio-economic status, relative to only 7 per cent in the CLHs. In the SGCH and CLH, the respondents with higher socio-economic status had 2.50 and 2.90 MLB for those with low socio-economic status.

Socio-economic status emerged as the most powerful determinant of fertility. All the socio-economic characteristics independently also had strong inverse relationship with fertility. Lower socio-economic status, especially in the case of child labour households, resulted in high fertility. It must be realised that literacy is prerequisite for attaining high occupational and economic status and for decreasing fertility. Planners and policy makers should keep this in view. Prevalence of low socio-economic status levels for a large proportion of CLHs and about one third of the SGCHs indicates the necessity for effective implementation of suitable rural development and educational programmes.

4

Demographic Characteristics and Fertility Behaviour

An unprecedented acceleration of population growth that has manifested in todays world has necessitated the study of the size, composition, characteristics and distribution of population, as it enables to look at the population situation scientifically. Knowledge of these demographic events is essential for the formulation of suitable developmental strategies as demographic variables have been reported to have a great impact on the determinants of family size in different cultures (*Driver*, 1963; *Mahadevan,* 1979). The present study, attempted to examine the effect of a few demographic variables on fertility.

Present Age of the Mother and Fertility

Age is a bio-social factor and present age of mother is one of the determinants of fertility behaviour. It is the main component of a population. Generally fertility is higher among the women in older age groups when compared to the younger groups, that is, as age of the mother increases fertility also increases in a non-contraceptive society.

It may be noted that almost equal percentage of women in both the groups belonged to the age group of 26-30 years and

36 + years. i.e., 24 per cent of SGCH and 21 per cent of CLH women were in the age group of 26-30 years and 31 per cent each of the SGCH and CLH women were above the age of 36 +. However, nearly one third of the CLH women were young, and below 25 years while nearly one third of the SGCH women were in the age group of 31-35 years.

Table—4.1. Percentage Distribution of School Going Children Households and Child Labour Households by Age of the Mother and Mean Live Births.

Present age of the mother	SGCH		CLH	
	%	MLB	%	MLB
25	18.00 (27)	2.67 (27)	29.33 (44)	3.22 (44)
26-30	24.00 (36)	2.83 (36)	21.33 (32)	3.83 (32)
31-35	27.33 (41)	3.17 (41)	18.00 (27)	4.25 (27)
36 +	30.67 (46)	3.21 (46)	31.34 (47)	4.37 (47)
Total	**100.00 (150)**	**3.01 (150)**	**100.00 (150)**	**3.84 (150)**

Present age of the mother was directly related to fertility. The data confirmed this positive relationship. As with the duration of marriage, here too, with the increase in age, the fertility also increased. It may be observed that the fertility of the SGCH women was lower in all the age groups compared to the CLH. In the age group 26-30 years, the CLH women had 1.00 MLB more than that of the SGCH women and this difference in fertility continued to increase with increase in age.

Age at Marriage and Fertility

Age at marriage is one of the major factors that determine fertility. Today, age at marriage is particularly important, because by 1990 there will be more than one billion young people of marriageable age (roughly in between 15 and 29 years) in the developing countries (population reports: No. 4, 1979). The decisions these young people make on marriage and child bearing will determine the population growth, for the years to come. Thus an analysis of the age at marriage is important for any fertility project.

Age at marriage correlates strongly with fertility in developing countries like India. In universally has an inverse relationship with fertility. i.e., higher the age at marriage lower the fertility and vice-versa.

Table—4.2. Percentage Distribution of School Going Children Households and Child Labour Households by Age at Marriage and Mean Live Births.

Age at marriage	SGCH		CLH	
	%	MLB	%	MLB
–15	9.33 (14)	3.83 (14)	27.33 (41)	4.17 (41)
16-17	20.67 (31)	3.39 (31)	36.00 (54)	3.96 (54)
18-19	40.00 (60)	2.86 (60)	26.67 (40)	3.58 (40)
20 +	30.00 (45)	2.63 (45)	10.00 (15)	3.21 (15)
Total	**100.00** **(150)**	**3.01** **(150)**	**100.00** **(150)**	**3.84** **(150)**

The data indicated significant differences between the school going children households and child labour households. Among the child labour families more than a quarter were married below 15 years of age and more than one third between 16 and 17 years of age. In contrast 70 per cent school going children households married above 18 years, which is the minimum legal age at marriage for girls.

Of this, 30 per cent were married above 20 years. About 10 per cent of school going children Households married below 15 years as against 10 per cent of child labour Households who married above 20 years of age.

The inverse relationship between age at marriage and fertility behaviour was confirmed. In both the sectors it may be observed that with increasing age at marriage, fertility decreased. At 15 years of age at marriage the fertility of school going children Households was 3.83—Mean live births, as against 2.63 MLB at 20 years of age at marriage. Among the child labour Households the corresponding figures were 4.17 MLB and 3.21 MLB. There was a decrease of 1.20 MLB with increasing age at marriage for SGCHs and 0.96 MLB for the CLHs. In general the decrease in fertility with increasing age at marriage was higher for the SGCH as compared to CLH.

The findings indicated that the age at marriage for more than half of the CLH and about one fifth of SGCH was low that is below 17 years. This is a general trend existing in most of the rural areas of Andhra Pradesh. If population growth is to be controlled as speedily as possible then, inevitably age at marriage has to be increased.

Duration of Marriage and Fertility

Duration of marriage is the most important determinant of fertility behaviour. The number of children concerned is dependent upon duration of marriage while all other factors remain constant. It is generally understood that women with longer duration of marriage have relatively more number of children compared to those with shorter duration of marital life. The findings of the SRS (Office of the Registrar General, India) conducted in 1972 covering the rural and urban married women in India also fully confirmed the direct positive relationships between duration of marriage and fertility.

Table—4.3. Percentage Distribution of School Going Children Households and Child Labour Households by Duration of Marriage and Mean Live Births.

Duration of Marriage	SGCH		CLH	
	%	MLB	%	MLB
–10	18.67 (28)	3.36 (28)	6.67 (10)	3.20 (10)
11-15	65.33 (98)	2.85 (98)	82.67 (124)	3.65 (124)
16 +	16.00 (24)	3.58 (24)	10.66 (16)	3.98 (16)
Total	**100.00 (150)**	**3.01 (150)**	**100.00 (150)**	**3.84 (150)**

A large proportion of the respondents irrespective of other differences had a marital life of 11-15 years. More than half of the SGCH and CLH had 11-15 years of marital union; though the percentage of respondents who had 11-15 years of married life was higher among the CLH. Negligible number of CLH (6%) had less than or equal to ten years of married life as against nearly one fifth of the SGCH (19%).

The data confirmed the direct relationship between duration of marriage and fertility behaviour. In both the sectors, fertility increased with increase in the duration of married life, though the increase in fertility was slightly more for the SGCH. In the SGCH group, the mean live births increased by 0.49 for those with 10 or less, years of marital life relative to those with 11-15 years. The corresponding figure for the CLH was 0.45. Thus, it may be observed that duration of marriage had positive relationship with fertility.

Breast Feeding and Fertility

Breast Feeding is a tradition among Indian women and the value of mothers milk as a form of infant feeding has been realised for over 2000 years. It is the safest and cleanest form of feeding. In poor communities, with people living in an unhygienic surroundings, milk especially bottle milk is liable for contamination resulting in bowel infections. Further, it is also a safe method of contraception. Would wide demographic investigation have confirmed the age old belief that breast feeding prolonged post-partiun amenorrhea and offered some degree of protection against pregnancy. Since this aspect also was relevant to value of children, (vide chapter V), the present study examined the relationship.

Table—4.4. Percentage Distribution School Going Children Households and Child Labour Households by Practice Breast Feeding and Mean Live Births.

Infant feeding	SGCH		CLH	
	%	MLB	%	MLB
Breast feeding	40.00 (60)	2.90 (60)	80.00 (120)	3.60 (120)
Others	60.00 (90)	3.12 (90)	20.00 (30)	4.08 (30)
Total	**100.00 (150)**	**3.01 (150)**	**100.00 (150)**	**3.84 (150)**

Many of the respondents were breast feeding their infants. Less than half of the SGCH (40%) and an overwhelming proportion of the CLH were breast feeding their infants. The respondents who were breast feeding their babies stated 1½ to 2 years as the mean duration of feeding and unanimously stated that breast feeding was the best for the health of the baby.

However, 60 per cent of SGCH were not breast feeding their infants. Majority stated that they had given breast milk to their baby upto three months but later on shifted to bottle feeding as they felt weak. This misconception and negative attitude to breast feeding, unfortunately seems to be prevalent more among the economically better off, which also seems to be plaguing the sample respondents also particularly to SGCH.

In contrast majority of the women in CLH were Breast feeding and stated 2½ to 3 years as the mean duration of feeding. Poor economic status may also be one of the causes for this. The reason for breast feeding the babies was that they had sufficient milk and it satisfied the hunger of the baby. This high mean duration of breast feeding practice among the CLH was a result of their poverty incapability on the part of the parents to provide sufficient supplementary food to the child.

The present data confirmed the depressing influence of breast feeding on fertility significantly. The MLB of the SGCH and CLH women who breast feed their infant was 2.90 and 3.60 as against 3.12 and 4.08 MLB respectively, of the respondents who resorted to other types of feeding practices the SGCH women who did not breast feed had 0.22 MLB more than those who breast feed their infants. The corresponding figure for the CLH sector was 0.48 MLB. The overall trend indicated that the respondents who resorted to breast feeding had fewer children relative to those who did not.

The findings of the study reflect the present trend of discontinuing breast feeding with the misconception that it spoils the figure and adversely affects health of the mother, in the SGCH group. However most of the women in CLH and some in SGCH breast feed their infants. Keeping in view the negative attitude towards breast feeding, it is necessary to advise the present and prospective mothers about the various health and contraceptive aspects of breast feeding.

Health Status and Fertility

Today, the awareness that the ultimate goal of development is to bring improvement in the quality of life has increased and as such health forms the integral and essential component of general development strategy.

Health status of the women and their fertility are strongly interrelated. Health status influences reproductive behaviour which in turn affects the health status. As such the health status of the wive's in both the sectors was analysed to study its effect on fertility and vice versa.

Table—4.5. Percentage Distribution of School Going Children Households and Child Labour Households by Health Status and Mean Live Births.

Health status	SGCH		CLH	
	%	MLB	%	MLB
Healthy	61.32 (92)	2.60 (92)	24.00 (36)	3.50 (36)
Unhealthy	38.68 (58)	3.42 (58)	76.00 (114)	4.18 (114)
Total	**100.00 (150)**	**3.01 (150)**	**100.00 (150)**	**3.84 (150)**

Significant differences may be observed in the health status of women in SGCHs and CLHs. More than 60 per cent of women in SGCH were healthy while only a quarter (24%) of the women in CLH reported so. Nearly three quarters of women in CLH stated that their health status was very poor. Of the women who were unhealthy, the predominant cause among the SGCH was Malaria (which was prevalent in this area), and common ailments like flu, colds and coughs etc. A negligible percentage of the women were anaemic.

In contrast, a quarter of the women, in CLH were anemic due to too may pregnancies (4 + children) and malnutrition. Further a large percentage of them were breast feeding their infants without taking proper balanced diet resulting in weakness. In this group too, more than a quarter of them were affected with malaria. One of the causes for the high incidence of Malaria in this area is unsanitary conditions in and around most of the households especially the CLH, breeding, mosquitoes.

Table—4.6. Percentage Distribution of School Going Children Households and Child Labour Households by Causes for Unhealth.

Causes for ill-health	SGCH %	CLH %
N.A	61.32 (92)	24.00 (36)
Common ailments	10.00 (15)	11.30 (17)
Anaemia	3.34 (5)	23.33 (35)
Malaria	12.00 (18)	26.70 (40)
General weakness	13.34 (20)	14.67 (22)
Total	**100.00 (150)**	**100.00 (150)**

The data showed that mothers who reported to be unhealthy had high fertility, in both the sectors suggesting that larger the family size, lower the health status. Similar trend existed in both the sectors through the fertility levels of the SGCH were lower than that of the CLH. Healthy mothers relative to the unhealthy, had 0.82 MLB less in the SGCH sector while the CLHs had 0.68 lower MLB. Thus, it is clear that the health status of the mother is adversely affected by high fertility.

In many instances, the relationship reflects the adverse effects of family over-crowding on the health status of the mother. On the other hand, a women with poor health is also not able to produce a healthy child. Miscarriages, abortions, infant mortality, nutritional deficiency of the child, mental and physical retardment are other possible adverse consequences. While an unhealthy mother makes the family miserable, her premature death makes living conditions appalling. On the other hand, an unhealthy child born to illness, before during and after pregnancy will also make the mother and the family suffer. In the sample area, also most of the children in the CLH, especially those whose mothers were unhealthy, were reported to suffer from high malnutrition, anaemia and general weakness.

The findings confirm the assumption that family planning is a rational means of reducing these risks, especially when it is made available in the context of maternal and child health.

Sum UP

Almost equal percentage of women in both the groups belonged to the age group of 26-30 years and 36 + years. Nearly one third of the CLH women were young, and below 25 years while nearly one third of the SGCH women were in the age group of 31-35 years. Present age of the mother was directly related to fertility. It may be observed that the fertility of the SGCH women was lower in all the age groups compared to the CLH. In the age group 26-30 years, the CLH women had 1.00 MLB more than that of the SGCH women and this difference in fertility continued to increase with increase in age. Among the child labour families more than a quarter were married below 15 years of age and more than one third between 16 and 17 years of age. In contrast 70 per cent school going children households married above 18 years, which is the minimum legal age at marriage for girls. Of this, 30 per cent were married above 20 years. In both the sectors, it may be observed that with increasing age at marriage, fertility decreased. There was a decrease of 1.20 MLB with increasing age at marriage for SGCH and 0.96 MLB for the CLHs.

A large proportion of the respondents irrespective of other differences had a marital life of 11-15 years. Negligible number of CLH (6%) had less than or equal to ten years of married life as against nearly one fifth of the SGCH (19%). The data confirmed the direct relationship between duration of marriage and fertility behaviour. In the SGCH group, the mean live births increased by 0.49 for those with 10 or less years of marital life relative to those with 11-15 years. The corresponding figure for the CLH was 0.45. Many of the respondents were breast feeding their infants. Less than half of the SGCH (40%) and an overwhelming proportion of the CLH were breast feeding their infants. The respondents who were breast feeding their babies stated 1½ to 2 years as the mean duration of feeding and unanimously stated that breast feeding was best for the health of the baby. In contrast, majority of the women in CLH were breast feeding and stated 2½ to 3 years as the mean duration of feeding. The reason for breast feeding the babies was that they had sufficient milk and it satisfied the hunger of the baby. The present data confirmed the depressing influence of breast feeding in fertility significantly. The MLB of the SGCH and CLH women who breast feed their infant was 2.90 and 3.60 as against 3.12 and 4.08 MLB respectively, of the respondents who restored to other types of feeding practices. More than 60 per cent of women in SGCH were healthy while only a quarter (24%) of the women in CLH reported so. Nearly three quarters of women in CLH stated that their health status was very poor. Of the women who were unhealthy, the predominant cause among the SGCH was Malaria. A quarter of the women in CLH were anemic due to too many pregnancies (4 + children) and malnutrition. In this group too, more than a quarter of them were affected with malaria. The data showed that mothers who reported to be unhealthy had high fertility, in both the sectors suggesting that larger the family size, lower the health status.

5

Perceived Benefits and Costs of Rearing Children

The systematic study of the value of children is relatively new. Before the introduction of effective contraceptive measures, it was meaningless even to discuss the problem of why people want and have children. Couples had very limited choice as to whether they would or would not have children or additional children. But, with effective contraceptives available, people can decide whether or not to have children and how many children they want to have. It is in this context that it becomes meaningful to ask why people want and have children, and how these reasons are related to their family size decisions.

In asking such questions, we are dealing with people's perceptions of the values of children and the interplay of positive (benefits and negative costs) values of children in relation to family size desires and decisions.

The "Value of children" refers to parents' perceptions of the satisfactions of having children and the perceived costs entailed in having children. In other words, basically two dimensions of the value of children are being examined here, the positive values or satisfactions or benefits and the negative values or costs. On a conceptual level, the value of children may be regarded as a balance between these two opposing forces, and it assumed that child bearing decisions depend on which of the two opposing forces dominates. As long as positive values outweigh negative values, parents will continue having children. Parents will presumably stop having children when the negative and positive values of children are at a balance, or particularly when negative values outweigh positive values. The numerical level of children at which parents stop is of special interest and significance demographically. The questions of how and why negative values dominate over positive values are particularly relevant. Answers to these questions are crucial to a complete understanding of fertility trends and decisions and also to the development of effective population policies.

Studies of the values placed on children in various western and non-western societies (*Fawcett and Arnold,* 1972; *Arnold et al.,* 1975; *For,* 1982) show that children constitute an important component of a happy and normal family life. They have concluded that in most of the societies, children have both economic and symbolic values and that such values are located with in an individual's total belief systems about marriage, family, quality and purpose of life. Consequently parents perceive the value of children in relation to their net social, economical, psychological and cultural benefits and losses.

In general, there are non-economic benefits (social, psychological, cultural etc.) and costs. Parent's perception of the non-economic benefits and costs of children and the extent and ways these perceptions influence family size decisions, and fertility are also of importance. Parents perception of the benefits and costs of children and the value they attach to these costs and benefits constitute their general attitude towards having children. In considering the relation between benefits and costs of children on the one hand and family size decisions and fertility on the other, therefore, it is important to know what parents general attitude towards children is.

This chapter discusses and analyses the benefits and costs of children as perceived by the SGCH, and CLHs. The study covers two broad categories of benefits and costs-economic and non-economic. An attempt is made to assess the extent to which these perceived benefits and costs of children are related to family size decisions and consequently to fertility.

Further, as it is difficult to measure and interpret perceived values of rearing children which are purely qualitative, an index combining all specific and related attitudinal statements has been adopted. This was considered a better methodological approach as measurement is bound to be improved when answers to several related questions are taken into account.

Perceived Economic Costs of Rearing Children

Perceived Economic costs of rearing children are the subjective perceptions of the parents, their sensitivity and attitude towards the various maintenance costs of rearing children. Those costs include perception of parents towards children as a financial burden, savings for children's future education, marriages, costs of child rearing precluding over all other purchases, preoccupation with child rearing as a cause for not working now and higher child costs as a cause for taking up employment etc.

In response to the various statements covering perceptions on economic costs of rearing children, a large per cent of the SGCH's confirmed that they were very much aware of the various economic costs involved in rearing children as against a smaller proportion of the CLH's. 60 to 80 per cent of the SGCHs stated that children were a heavy financial burden, children's education was a worry, children were expensive to feed and cloth, a large number of children (4 +) lead to too many divisions of property and made the family less well-off, resulted in increasing financial problems in future and that dowry to be given during a daughter's marriage—were important costs which had definite influence on family size decision's. In contrast, only heavy financial burden, children's educational costs, expenditure on food and dowry for performing daughter's marriage were cited by CLH's.

Table—5.1. Percentage Distribution and Mean Live Birth of SCHs and CLHs by Perceived Economic Costs of Rearing Children.

Statements	Agree				Uncertain				Disagree			
	SCH		CLH		SCH		CLH		SCH		CLH	
	%	MLB	%	MLB	%	MLB	%	MLB	%	MLB	%	MLB
1	2	3	4	5	6	7	8	9	10	11	12	13
1. Raising children is a heavy financial burden for most people	80.00 (120)	2.96 (120)	65.33 (98)	3.79 (98)	—	—	—	—	20.00 (30)	3.23 (30)	34.67 (52)	3.92 (52)
2. The real financial worry about children is their education	68.00 (102)	2.90 (102)	75.33 (113)	3.78 (113)	—	—	—	—	32.00 (48)	3.25 (48)	24.67 (37)	4.02 (37)
3. Children eat very little but they are still expensive	64.00 (96)	2.95 (96)	77.33 (116)	3.76 (116)	8.00 (12)	3.00 (12)	4.67 (7)	3.86 (7)	28.00 (42)	3.14 (42)	18.00 (27)	4.15 (27)
4. Clothing of children is a financial worry	62.67 (94)	2.98 (94)	45.33 (68)	3.72 (68)	37.33 (56)	3.07 (56)	54.67 (82)	3.93 (82)	—	—	—	—
5. Housing is a problem when there are more children	56.00 (84)	3.03 (84)	47.33 (71)	3.80 (71)	—	—	4.00 (6)	3.83 (6)	44.00 (66)	2.98 (66)	44.00 (73)	3.87 (73)

(Contd...)

Table—5.1 (Contd...)

1	2	3	4	5	6	7	8	9	10	11	12	13
6. Too many children means too many divisions of property	64.00 (96)	2.82 (96)	42.00 (63)	3.73 (63)	—	—	—	—	36.00 (54)	3.37 (54)	58.00 (87)	3.91 (87)
7. Having lot of children will make their families less well-off	62.00 (93)	2.80 (93)	36.00 (54)	3.91 (54)	12.67 (19)	3.00 (19)	60.00 (90)	3.80 (90)	25.33 (38)	3.21 (38)	4.00 (6)	3.97 (6)
8. The only worry about daughters is about their marriage and dowry	72.00 (108)	2.98 (108)	62.00 (93)	3.73 (93)	9.67 (14)	3.01 (14)	5.67 (8)	3.75 (8)	24.33 (38)	3.14 (38)	32.33 (49)	3.92 (49)
9. Having many and frequent pregnancies means increased financial problems later on in life	76.67 (115)	2.98 (115)	51.67 (77)	3.81 (77)	—	—	—	—	23.33 (35)	3.11 (35)	48.33 (73)	3.87 (73)
10. Having many children restricts occupational mobility	42.00 (56)	2.80 (56)	38.67 (58)	3.70 (58)	58.00 (94)	3.13 (94)	61.33 (92)	3.92 (92)	—	—	—	—

Of the various costs which were mentioned as significant, financial burden of rearing children in the present, increased financial problems in future and providing dowry for the daughters were cited as very important in a high percentage of the SGCHs. On the other hand, among the CLH's cost of feeding and educating children were considered as very important. In this context, it would be apt to state the opinion of *Bulatao* (1982)—the actual costs of maintaining children may not be much in pleasant settings but relative to incomes these costs are considerable and extremely significant and are generally the most mentioned costs.

Further, the percentage of respondents who were unaware of certain costs of rearing children like occupational immobility, clothing of children is a worry, makes a family less well-off etc. and hence were uncertain were more among the CLH's.

Index on Perceived Economic Costs of Rearing Children

Index on perceived economic costs of rearing children was constructed by allotting numerical values to the opinion of respondents: 3 for agreement, 2 for uncertain, 1 for disagree—on all the items of perceived economic costs of rearing children. These values were further grouped into three categories. The first category with 10-16, indicated low status, 17-23 is second category and 24-30 is the third category which indicated high status.

Significant differences existed between the SGCH's and CLHs. The overall trend confirmed that various economic costs of rearing children influenced the fertility decisions. 40 per cent of the SGCH who had higher perception of economic costs of children had lower fertility (2.83); while 12 per cent had lower perception of economic costs of rearing children and had higher fertility (3.22).

In general, the fertility of the child labour households was higher than that of SGCHs. More than a quarter of the CLHs who had very low perception of economic costs of rearing children had higher MLB (4.08). 30 per cent of the CLHs having high perception of economic costs of children had lower fertility (3.62). Majority (56%) of the CLHs had moderate or average perception of economic costs of rearing children and had 3.90 mean live births.

Table—5.2. Percentage Distribution of the School Going Children Households and Child Labour Households by Index of Perceived Economic Costs of Rearing Children and Mean Live Births.

Index	SGCH		CLH	
	%	MLB	%	MLB
Low	12.00 (18)	3.22 (18)	26.00 (39)	4.08 (39)
Medium	48.00 (72)	3.11 (72)	56.00 (81)	3.90 (81)
High	40.00 (60)	2.83 (60)	20.00 (30)	3.62 (30)
Total	**100.00 (150)**	**3.01 (150)**	**100.00 (150)**	**3.84 (150)**

It may be observed that the percentage of respondents who were greatly aware of the various costs and stated so was more among the SGCH than the CLHs. Further, it may be noted that perception of various dimensions of cost of rearing children influenced the family size decisions and fertility behaviour.

Perceived Non-economic Costs of Rearing Children

Perceived non-economic costs of rearing children are the emotional and physical demands made by children on their parents. They are costs like noise and disorder in the house, extra housework, general weariness to the mother, lack of time, privacy, sleep and worry to the parents and such other costs i.e., adverse affects of a large number of children (4 +) on the well-being of a household.

Table—5.3. Percentage Distribution and Mean Live Births of SCHs and CLHs by Perceived Non-Economic Costs of Rearing Children.

Statements	Agree				Uncertain				Disagree			
	SCH		CLH		SCH		CLH		SCH		CLH	
	%	MLB	%	MLB	%	MLB	%	MLB	%	MLB	%	MLB
1	2	3	4	5	6	7	8	9	10	11	12	13
1. Many children means extra work care	78.67 (118)	2.97 (118)	50.67 (76)	3.82 (76)	9.00 (12)	3.00 (12)	7.33 (11)	3.81 (11)	13.33 (20)	3.30 (20)	42.00 (63)	3.87 (63)
2. Many children is a weary and tedious jobs	70.66 (106)	2.80 (106)	62.67 (94)	3.68 (94)	6.67 (10)	3.20 (10)	5.33 (8)	3.87 (8)	22.67 (34)	3.61 (34)	32.00 (48)	4.14 (48)
3. Having many children is a great mental strain and loss of sleep	85.33 (128)	2.92 (128)	64.00 (96)	3.77 (96)	4.00 (6)	3.00 (6)	8.67 (13)	4.00 (13)	10.67 (16)	3.25 (16)	27.33 (41)	3.96 (41)
4. Having many children means less leisure	70.00 (105)	3.00 (105)	62.00 (93)	3.88 (93)	—	—	10.00 (15)	3.86 (15)	30.00 (45)	3.04 (45)	28.00 (42)	3.83 (42)
5. Having many children causes problems and dis-agreements between wife and husband	61.33 (92)	2.96 (92)	55.33 (83)	3.62 (83)	—	—	—	—	38.67 (58)	3.10 (58)	44.67 (67)	4.11 (67)

1	2	3	4	5	6	7	8	9	10	11	12	13
6. Many children leads to loss of affection between the couple	58.00 (87)	2.82 (87)	52.00 (78)	3.77 (78)	12.00 (18)	2.88 (18)	16.00 (24)	3.83 (24)	30.00 (45)	3.44 (45)	32.00 (48)	3.96 (48)
7. Many pregnancies results in deterioration of mother's health	74.66 (112)	2.98 (112)	61.33 (92)	3.82 (92)	10.67 (16)	3.00 (16)	14.67 (22)	3.84 (22)	14.67 (22)	3.14 (22)	28.00 (42)	3.98 (42)
8. Too many children means lack of privacy	55.33 (80)	2.92 (80)	45.33 (68)	3.68 (68)	44.67 (70)	3.11 (70)	55.67 (82)	3.97 (82)	—	—	—	—
9. Having many children does not permit the wife to have contacts and friendships outside the home and participate in community development activities	57.33 (86)	3.00 (86)	50.67 (76)	3.74 (76)	—	—	—	—	42.67 (64)	3.03 (64)	49.33 (74)	3.94 (74)
10. Many children restrict social life (eg., can not attend marriages, parties, meetings etc.)	62.00 (93)	2.88 (93)	48.67 (73)	3.77 (73)	30.00 (45)	3.18 (45)	51.33 (77)	3.91 (77)	9.00 (12)	3.41 (12)	—	—

Significant differences may be observed between the SGCH and CLH regarding their perception of non-economic costs of rearing children as well as their fertility levels. A large proportion of the SGCH (60-85 per cent) cited that restrictions on social life, determination of mother's health, problems between spouses, less leisure, great mental strain, more physical work, tedious and weary work were highly salient costs of rearing children. As against this 60 to 65 per cent of CLH's stated that Mental strain weary and tedious work, less leisure and deterioration of mother's health as important non-economic costs of rearing children. However, in both the groups, the mental strain, physical burden and tediousness involved in rearing children, deterioration of mother's health due to too many pregnancies were cited as the most important.

Further, the fertility of the respondents who agreed with these costs of rearing children was lower, in both the groups. The data suggests that in addition to money, children consume parents time and sap their physical energy, imposing great mental strain. Some of the sacrifices parents have to make may be in the form of giving up employment while it is mostly in the form of lost sleep, lost leisure, heavy physical and mental strain. The awareness of these costs arising from rearing of more number of children, negatively influences family size decisions resulting in transition in the values of children and thus lower fertility.

Index on Perceived Non-economic Costs of Rearing Children

An index on perceived non-economic costs of rearing children was developed by allotting numerical values to the opinion of the respondents— 3 for agree, 2 for uncertain and 1 for disagree on each statement with regard to non-economic costs of rearing children. Highest value was assigned for agree and lowest value for disagree over non-economic costs of rearing children. Accordingly three categories were formed the first category of 10-16 scores indicated lowest values and last category of 24-30 scores highest values.

Table—5.4. Percentage Distribution of the School Going Children Households and Child Labour Households by Index Perceived Non-economic Costs of Rearing Children and Mean Live Births.

Index	SGCH		CLH	
	%	MLB	%	MLB
Low	7.33 (11)	3.18 (11)	27.33 (41)	3.68 (41)
Medium	52.00 (78)	3.07 (78)	62.00 (93)	3.86 (93)
High	40.67 (61)	2.95 (61)	10.67 (16)	4.12 (16)
Total	**100.00** **(150)**	**3.01** **(150)**	**100.00** **(150)**	**3.84** **(150)**

SGCHs and CLHs differed significantly in relation to their perception of non-economic costs of rearing children. The data showed that 41 per cent of the SGCH and about one-fifth of the CLHs agreed on most aspects on non-economic costs and stated that rearing many children (4 +) adversely affected parents lives. A higher proportion of the respondents among SGCH (52%) relative to CLHs (62%) had moderate perception. Of the remaining respondents, 7.3 per cent SGCH relative to 27 per cent of the CLH disagreed with these costs.

The overall trend confirmed the hypothesis that various aspects of non-economic costs of rearing children affected fertility behaviour. The data revealed that the fertility of the SGCHs was lower than the child labour households. The respondents among the SGCHs and CLHs who disagreed over the influence of non-economic costs and scored low on this index and had 3.18 and 4.12 mean live births as against those who agreed with these costs and scored "high" on the cost index and had a low fertility of 2.95 and 3.68 mean live births respectively. The findings showed that both among the SGCHs and CLHs the fertility of the respondents declined with increase in the perception of non-economic costs of rearing children.

Perceived Economic Benefits of Rearing Children

Off late, economic benefits from children have attracted the attention of researchers. The idea of having children because of the economic contributions they can make seem strange and ridiculous to parents in developed countries faced with the considerable costs of feeding, clothing, educating, medicating and entertaining children. But it is a common consideration among rural households in many developing countries where children as young as six years, start to help parents in the fields and in the house. Chores such as tending livestock, collecting firewood and caring for younger children are commonly assigned to youngsters. In addition, most parents expect to recover their investment in children by receiving support from them in old age.

It may be seen that confirming to the general feeling that economic benefits from children play an important role, a large per cent of the CLH's (65-85%) cited almost all the economic benefits of rearing children as salient. Even benefits like children are inheritors of property and reliable hands to maintain wealth have been cited by more than half of the child labour households.

Almost all the benefits were cited as important by school going children households also, but to a far lesser extent. As such, differences in perception on the economic benefits of rearing children between the CLHs and SGCHs were reflected in their fertility levels also. The fertility of the child labour households was higher as their positive perception of economic benefits from children were more against the school going children households whose fertility was relatively lower due to disagreement by majority regarding the economic benefits to be obtained by having many children.

The findings suggested that parents do perceive that children make significant economic contributions to the family.

Table—5.5. Percentage Distribution and Mean Live Births of SCHs and CLHs by Perceived Economic Benefits of Rearing Children.

Statements	Agree				Uncertain				Disagree			
	SCH		CLH		SCH		CLH		SCH		CLH	
	%	MLB	%	MLB	%	MLB	%	MLB	%	MLB	%	MLB
1	2	3	4	5	6	7	8	9	10	11	12	13
1. Without young children help men would find it difficult to do their farm, businesses work	60.67 (91)	3.22 (91)	72.00 (108)	3.98 (108)	6.00 (9)	2.89 (9)	3.33 (5)	3.80 (5)	33.33 (50)	2.84 (50)	24.66 (37)	3.76 (37)
2. Without unmarried daughter's help women would find it difficult to do their house work	57.33 (86)	3.15 (86)	74.67 (112)	3.88 (112)	4.00 (6)	3.00 (6)	5.33 (8)	3.75 (8)	38.67 (58)	2.81 (58)	20.00 (30)	3.73 (30)
3. A good reason for having children is that they can help when parents are too old to work	68.00 (102)	3.16 (102)	80.67 (121)	3.90 (121)	—	—	—	—	32.00 (48)	2.71 (48)	19.33 (29)	3.62 (29)

(Contd...)

Table—5.5 (Contd...)

	1	2	3	4	5	6	7	8	9	10	11	12	13
4.	Children provide facilities required for meeting the physical needs and comforts of the parents in old age	61.33 (92)	3.12 (92)	65.33 (98)	3.88 (98)	18.00 (27)	2.96 (27)	24.00 (36)	3.83 (36)	20.67 (31)	2.71 (31)	10.67 (16)	3.62 (16)
5.	Inherit family property	52.67 (79)	3.09 (79)	54.00 (81)	3.99 (81)	—	—	8.00 (12)	3.75 (12)	47.33 (71)	2.93 (71)	38.00 (57)	3.65 (57)
6.	The best property a widow can have is children	74.67 (112)	3.09 (112)	82.00 (123)	3.87 (123)	6.00 (9)	2.88 (9)	12.00 (18)	3.72 (18)	19.33 (29)	2.76 (29)	6.00 (9)	3.66 (9)
7.	More children means large number of reliable hands to maintain wealth	45.33 (68)	3.22 (68)	56.00 (84)	4.00 (84)	25.33 (38)	2.76 (38)	30.67 (46)	3.65 (46)	29.33 (44)	2.91 (44)	13.33 (20)	3.60 (20)
8.	More sons means more dowries	42.00 (63)	3.13 (63)	82.00 (123)	3.87 (123)	37.33 (56)	2.98 (56)	12.00 (18)	3.72 (18)	20.67 (31)	2.84 (31)	6.00 (9)	3.57 (9)

Those perceptions of significant economic benefits are largely concentrated in the backward rural areas among the lower income groups and among child labour oriented families.

Index on Perceived Economic Benefits of Rearing Children

An Index of perceived economic benefits (Values) of rearing children was prepared by allotting numerical values to the opinion of respondents—1 for disagreement, 2 for uncertainty and 3 for agreement—on all the items of perceived economic benefits from children. Lowest value was assigned to negative response and highest value to positive response on perceived economic benefits from children.

Table—5.6. Percentage Distribution of the School Going Children Households and Child Labour Households by Index on Perceived Economic Benefits of Rearing Children and Mean Live Births.

Index	SGCH		CLH	
	%	MLB	%	MLB
High	28.67 (43)	3.15 (43)	77.33 (116)	3.89 (116)
Medium	13.33 (20)	3.05 (20)	4.66 (7)	3.86 (7)
Low	58.00 (87)	2.72 (87)	18.00 (27)	3.63 (27)
Total	**100.00 (150)**	**3.01 (150)**	**100.00 (150)**	**3.84 (150)**

From the data, it is evident that the respondents among the SGCH differed significantly from the CLHs in relation to their perception on economic benefits of rearing children. The data confirmed the hypothesis that perceived benefits from children were associated with large family.

The data indicated that about 58 per cent and 13 per cent of the SGCH scored 'Low' and 'Medium' on the index of perceived economic benefits of rearing children. The corresponding figure for CLHs was 77 per cent and 4.5 per cent respectively. They strongly cited a number of benefits from children. In contrast, 29 per cent of the SGCH and about 18 per cent of the child labour households stated that they have disagreed with these statements. The results clearly indicate strong positive relationship between economic benefits and fertility.

The data confirmed that respondents who perceive high economic benefits from their children had higher fertility. Among the SGCHs those who agreed that children had economic utility had higher mean live births (3.15). Their counterparts in CLHs and 3.89 MLB. The respondents who perceived low economic benefits from their children had lower fertility. Among the SGCH and CLHs who disagree about the influence of economic benefits and scored low on this index had a low fertility of 2.72 and 3.63 Mean live births respectively.

Thus the perception of economic benefits from children was a significant predicator of fertility variations.

Perceived Non-economic Benefits of Rearing Children

Perceived non-economic benefits of rearing children consist of social and psychological values as a source of joy and happiness, as a bond between husband and wife, fulfillment of marriage, attainment of adult-status and social prestige and extension of social relations, and in the form of cultural values such as carrying on the family name, fulfilling of religious obligations, performance of rituals, funeral rites etc.

Among the SGCHs, 60 to 80 per cent of the respondents cited most of the non-economic benefits of rearing children as significant kinship relation, family lineage and continuity, funeral rites, extension of social relations, Pride in children accomplishments were said to be very important, followed by more than half of the SGCHs who opined that the remaining

Table—5.7. Percentage Distribution and Mean Live Births of the Respondents by Perceived Non-Economic Values of Rearing Children.

Statements	Agree				Uncertain				Disagree			
	SCH		CLH		SCH		CLH		SCH		CLH	
	%	MLB	%	MLB	%	MLB	%	MLB	%	MLB	%	MLB
1	2	3	4	5	6	7	8	9	10	11	12	13
1. Give and take of love and affection	64.00 (96)	3.11 (96)	54.67 (82)	3.92 (82)	16.00 (24)	2.83 (24)	12.00 (18)	3.77 (18)	20.00 (30)	2.61 (30)	33.33 (50)	3.62 (50)
2. Enlarge kinship relation	78.67 (118)	3.08 (118)	82.67 (124)	3.87 (124)	6.00 (9)	2.77 (9)	7.33 (11)	3.81 (11)	15.33 (23)	2.74 (23)	10.00 (15)	3.67 (15)
3. Continuity family line (Lineage)	70.00 (105)	3.10 (105)	88.00 (132)	3.89 (132)	4.00 (6)	2.83 (6)	5.33 (8)	3.75 (8)	26.00 (39)	2.69 (39)	6.67 (10)	3.70 (10)
4. Perform rituals in the family	56.00 (84)	3.16 (84)	63.33 (98)	3.92 (98)	12.00 (18)	3.00 (18)	17.33 (26)	3.77 (26)	32.00 (48)	2.71 (48)	17.33 (26)	3.69 (26)

(Contd...)

Table—5.7 (Contd...)

1	2	3	4	5	6	7	8	9	10	11	12	13
5. A person with children is respected in the community more than a person without children	55.33 (83)	3.21 (83)	61.33 (92)	3.88 (92)	8.00 (12)	2.84 (12)	12.00 (18)	3.80 (18)	36.67 (55)	2.76 (55)	26.67 (40)	3.65 (40)
6. One of the best things about having children is that you are never lonely	50.67 (76)	3.26 (76)	69.33 (104)	3.92 (104)	49.33 (74)	2.76 (74)	30.67 (46)	3.65 (46)	—	—	—	—
7. Perform funeral rites	72.67 (109)	3.12 (109)	78.67 (118)	3.89 (118)	14.00 (21)	2.86 (21)	16.00 (24)	3.60 (24)	13.33 (20)	2.70 (20)	5.33 (8)	3.70 (8)
8. Pride in children's accomplishments	65.33 (98)	3.18 (98)	69.33 (104)	3.92 (104)	6.00 (9)	2.88 (9)	10.00 (15)	3.67 (15)	28.67 (43)	2.65 (43)	20.67 (31)	3.68 (31)
9. Extension of social relation	74.67 (112)	3.09 (112)	77.33 (116)	3.93 (116)	—	—	8.00 (12)	3.75 (12)	25.33 (38)	2.79 (38)	14.67 (22)	3.60 (22)
10. Increase of social prestige through children states	52.00 (78)	3.28 (78)	58.67 (88)	4.00 (88)	8.67 (13)	3.00 (13)	9.33 (14)	3.71 (14)	39.33 (59)	2.66 (59)	32.00 (48)	3.58 (48)

non-economic benefits of rearing children like performance of rituals, social sanctions, prestige in society and companionship were also significant. In the CLH's all the costs were stated as salient by more than 65 per cent of the respondents. More than three quarter of them opined that Kinship relations, family lineage and continuity, performance of rituals in the family, funeral rites, prestige in society, companionship, extension of social relations and pride in children accomplishments were significant non-economic values of rearing children. Compared to the SGCHs, the CLHs perceived higher non-economic benefits from children, and as such this trend was reflected in their fertility levels.

The CLHs, in general, had higher fertility than the SGCHs. However within the groups, those who perceived higher non-economic benefits from children had higher fertility. Strong positive relationships between fertility and non-economic values of children may be observed in both the groups.

Index on Perceived Non-economic Values of Children

An index of perceived non-economic values of rearing children was constructed by allotting numerical values to the opinions of the respondents— 1 for disagree, 2 for uncertain and 3 for agree—for each statement with regard to non-economic benefits from children. Lowest value was assigned to the negative response and highest value to the positive response. Accordingly three categories were formed—the first category with 10-16 indicated lowest values and the last category with 24-30 indicated the highest values.

The SGCH and CLH significantly differed in relation to their perception on non-economic benefits from children. The trend indicated that more than half of the SGCH (52) scored low on the benefit index relative to 26 per cent of the CLH. Relatively 42 per cent of the SGCH and 64 per cent of CLH had scored high on the index on perceived non-economic benefits of children.

Table—5.8. Percentage Distribution of School Going Children Households and Child Labour Households by Index on Perceived Non-economic Benefits of Children and Mean Live Births.

Index	SGCH		CLH	
	%	MLB	%	MLB
High	42.00 (63)	3.14 (63)	64.00 (96)	3.91 (96)
Medium	5.33 (8)	3.12 (8)	10.00 (15)	3.90 (15)
Low	52.67 (79)	2.84 (79)	26.00 (39)	3.67 (39)
Total	**100.00 (150)**	**3.01 (150)**	**100.00 (150)**	**3.84 (150)**

The overall trend confirmed the hypothesis that the perceived non-economic benefits of rearing children affected fertility decisions. It may be observed that the respondents perceived benefits of rearing children was positively associated with their fertility. The fertility levels of the SGCH was less than that of CLHs. The Mean live births of the SGCHs who agreed with these perceived non-economic benefits and scored 'high' on this index was 3.14 as against CLHs who had 3.91 MLBs. Both SGCH and CLHs who did not agree with these perceived benefits and scored 'Low' on this index had a lowered fertility of 2.84 and 3.67 mean live births respectively.

Sum UP

In response to the various statements covering perceptions on economic costs of rearing children, a large per cent of the SGCH's confirmed that they were very much aware of the various economic costs involved in rearing children as against a smaller proportion of the CLH's. Of the various costs which were mentioned as significant, financial burden of rearing children, in the present, increased financial problems in future and providing dowry for the daughter were cited as very important in a high percentage of the SGCH's. On the other hand, among the CLH's cost of feeding and educating children were considered as very important. The overall trend confirmed that various economic costs of rearing children influenced the fertility decisions. 40 per cent of the SGCHs who had higher perception of economic costs of children had lower fertility (2.83); while 12 per cent had lower perception of economic costs of rearing children and had higher fertility (3.22).

The percentage of respondents who were greatly aware of the various costs and stated so was more among the SGCHs than the CLHs. Further, it may be noted that perception of various dimensions of cost of rearing children influenced the family size decisions and fertility behaviour.

Significant differences may be observed between the SGCH and CLH regarding their perception of non-economic costs of rearing children as well as their fertility levels. A large proportion of the SGCH (60-85%) cited that restrictions on social life, determination of mothers health, problems between spouses, less leisure, great mental strain, more physical work, tedious and weary work were highly salient costs of rearing children. As against this 60 to 65 per cent of CLH's stated that mental strain weary and tedious work, less leisure and deterioration of mothers health as important non-economic costs of rearing children. The fertility of the respondents who agreed with these costs of rearing children was lower, in both the groups. The awareness of these costs arising from rearing of more number of children, negatively influences family size decisions resulting in transition in the values of children and thus lower fertility. The data revealed that the fertility of the SGCH was lower than the child labour households. The respondents among the SGCHs and CLHs who disagreed over the influence of non-economic costs and scored low on this index and had 3.18 and 4.12 mean live births as against those who agreed with these costs and scored "high" on the cost index and had a low fertility of 2.95 and 3.68 mean live births respectively.

It may be seen that confirming to the general feeling that economic benefits from children play an important role, a large per cent of the CLH's (65-85%) cited almost all the economic benefits of rearing children as salient. Even benefits like children are inheritors of property and reliable hands to maintain wealth have been cited by more than half of the child labour households. Almost all the benefits were cited as important by school going children households also, but to a far lesser extent. The findings suggested that parents do perceive that children make significant economic contributions to the family. About 58 per cent and 13 per cent of the SGCHs scored 'Low' and 'Medium' on the index of perceived economic benefits of rearing children. The corresponding figure for CLHs was 77 per cent respectively. They strongly cited a number of benefits from children. In contrast, 29 per cent of the SGCH and about 18 per cent of the child labour households stated that they have disagreed with these statements. Among the SGCHs those who agreed that children had economic utility had higher mean live births (3.15). Their counterparts in CLHs had 3.89 MLB. Thus the perception of economic benefits from children was a significant predictor of fertility variations.

Among the SGCHs, 60 to 80 per cent of the respondents cited most of the non-economic benefits of rearing children as significant Kinship relation, family lineage and continuity, funeral rites extension of social relations, pride in children accomplishments were said to be very important. In the CLH's, all the costs were stated as salient by more than 65 per cent of the respondents. The CLHs, in general, had higher fertility than the SGCHs. However within the groups, those who perceived higher non-economic benefits from children had higher fertility. Strong positive relationships between fertility and non-economic values of children may be observed in both the groups. More than half of the SGCH (52) scored low on the benefit index relative to 26 per cent of the CLH. Relatively 42 per cent of the SGCH and 64 per cent of CLH had scored high on the index on perceived non-economic benefits of children. The mean live births of the

SGCHs who agreed with these perceived non-economic benefits and scored 'high' on this index was 3.14 as against CLHs who had 3.91 MLBs. Both SGCH and CLHs who did not agree with these perceived benefits and scored 'Low' on this index had a lower fertility of 2.84 and 3.67 mean live births respectively.

The SGCHs and CLHs differed significantly in relation to their perceptions on all the aspects of benefits and costs of rearing children. Majority of the SGCHs scored 'high' on the indices of economic and non-economic costs and 'low' on the indices of economic and non-economic benefits of rearing children, and thus had lower fertility relative to the CLHs. This may be due to the better socio-economic status levels of the SGCHs which may have influenced their attitude towards various values of children, rationalising their fertility decisions to have a small number of high quality children.

Thus, it is clear from the evidence provided by this study that various costs of rearing children have negative and various benefits have positive influences on the fertility behaviour of the couples. Hence, government should take steps to improve the socio-economic status levels of the rural households through effective implementation of rural development programmes. It should further emphasis the quality of the child in relation to small family size and increase the awareness of people that a few well educated and well placed children will be better able to realize the hopes of the parents.

6

Child Labour and Fertility Behaviour

Child labour contributes to the households income directly and indirectly. Children's work at home, on the family farm and in the family business, and their intangible contributions to the households income; whereas when they work outside the family enterprise, for returns in cash and kind, they supplement their family income in real terms. As such, the economic activities of children add to their economic values to parents in rural societies. They regard them as productive agents and hence as assets to the family. The more the number of children a family has got, the stronger it becomes financially is the prevailing belief. (A rural family, therefore, prefers to have large number of children expecting each one of them to work and add to the family income. High fertility is thus the chief consequence of child labour.)

(Past research on fertility has taken into account the role of children as an element in fertility decision making of couples.) Some studies on economic activities of children (*Schultz,* 1974; *Usha Rani,* 1989; *Naidu,* 1988; *Caldwell,* 1976) have found that child labour significantly contributes to the household production and that it cannot be denied that the tangible contribution of children to household income has a major role to play in the fertility decision making of couples. (As such in most agrarian societies, where the cost of bearing and rearing of children is low, and where children enter into labour force at an early age, a surviving child seems to be good asset. But in the Indian context, only a few fragmentary pieces of evidence are available on this subject. Hence, (the present chapter focusses on the labour value of children and its relationship with fertility. An attempt is made to present the dimensions, causes and consequences of child labour in two sections.)

Section 1 deals with actual child labour and section 2 with perceived value of child labour. The first section on Actual Child labour assessed only the CLH sector as only they had children in the labour force; while both sectors—CLH and SGCH—were assessed to examine the perceived labour value of children in the second section.

SECTION 1

Actual Child Labour Force Participation

Expectation of Income from Children

In order to find out the causes leading to the prevalence of child labour, the parents of children in the labour force i.e. CLHs were asked, if they had wanted their children to supplement to the family income by working.

Table—6.1. Percentage Distribution of Child Labour Households by Desire for Income from Children through Employment.

Response	Child labour households	
	No.	%
Yes	102	68
No	48	32
Total	**150**	**100**

(An overwhelmingly large proportion of the respondents in the CLH's stated that they had wanted their children to supplement to family income and hence had engaged them in the labour force.) Only 30 per cent of them said that they did not want their children to supplement to their income, but due to poverty and difficulty in making both the ends meet, the children had to work.

Source of Motivation

The parents of the child labourers were further asked to state whether they had motivated their children to work or did the children volunteer to work.

Table—6.2. Percentage Distribution, of the Child Labour Households by Source of Motivation for Child Labour

Source of motivation	Child labour households	
	No.	%
Parents	93	62
Volunteer	57	38
Total	**150**	**100**

As indicated in Table—6.1, here also the data showed that a large proportion of the parents wanted their children to earn and supplement to the family income and as such they motivated their children to join the labour force. However, nearly 40 per cent of the parents stated that their children volunteered to take up employment and thus help the households finances.

The findings clearly revealed that (majority of the parents viewed children as a form of asset, and expected them to work earn and supplement the household income.)

Age at which the Children had Started Work

The respondents were asked to state the age when their children have started working.

Table—6.3. Percentage Distribution of Child Labour Households by Age at which their Children had Started Work.

Age	Child labour households	
	No.	%
6	24	16
7-10	112	75
11-14	14	9
Total	**150**	**100**

A large percentage of the respondents stated that their children started working at a very young age. Only a negligible percentage of the parents said that their children started working after the age of 11 years. (Three fourths of the parents stated that their children started working in between the ages of 7 and 10 years, while slightly less than one fifth (16%) of them stated that their children started work below or at the age of 6 years.) All the respondents felt that from the age of 5 onwards, children are capable of undertaking small household chores and by the age of seven to eight become capable of economic returns.

Man Months Worked Per Annum by the Children

The respondents in the child labour household were asked to state the number of months the children worked in a year, in order to find out if the children were engaged throughout the year, even during agriculture off-season period.

(More than half of the respondents stated that their children worked for ten to twelve months in a year followed by about one third who said that they were engaged in economic activities for a period of seven to nine months.) Against this a little more than one tenth of the parents stated that their children were working for less than or equal to six months. However, the general trend

Table—6.4. Percentage Distribution of Child Labour Households by Man Months Worked by Children.

Man Months	Child labour households	
	No.	%
6	21	55
7-9	47	31
10-12	82	55
Total	**150**	**100**

that prevailed in this area, indicated that in the agricultural busy season, (all the children were employed at high wage rates but during the off-season they were engaged to carry on miscellaneous activities at slightly lower wage rates.) Majority of the parents send their children to work round the year at the going wage rates rather than have them idle even for a few months.

Wages Paid to the Children

The respondents were asked to state the average daily wages paid to their children.

Table—6.5. Percentage Distribution of Child Labour Households by Average Daily Wages Paid to Children.

Wages per day (in Rs.)	Child labour households	
	No.	%
7	18	12
8-12	48	32
13	84	56
Total	**150**	**100**

(More than half of the respondents stated that their children were paid Rs. 13/- on an average while on third were paid Rs. 8-12 per day.) A little more than one fifth of the children were paid Rs. 7/- per day on average. This trend is consistent with the data in Table—6.7 which shows that most of the children were employed as workers, animal herdsmen who were paid the highest wages followed by agricultural labourers.

Reason for Child Labour Force Participation

Several factors are said to be causes for child labour participation in economic activities such as poverty, caste, tradition, family size, labour security, wage rates, illiteracy, inadequate schooling facilities etc. All these factors are inter-linked and exert their influence directly and indirectly on the work participation of children. The respondents in the child labour households were asked to state the reasons for sending their children to work at a very young age.

Table—6.6. Percentage Distribution of Child Labour Households by Reasons for Sending Children to Work.

Reasons	Child labour households	
	No.	%
Poverty	67	45
Large family size	38	25
High wage rates	28	19
Inadequate schooling facilities	17	11
Total	**150**	**100**

The data highlights the fact that (for nearly fifty per cent of the respondents, poverty was the main cause for sending their children to work for wages.) Poverty compels millions of rural households to sell the labour of their children along with adults to eke out a bare subsistence. Further, poverty leads to indebtedness. Adult members of indebted households can neither save to clear of their debts nor can they leave their existing activities and work under the creditor to pay them off, for their present earnings are essential for family survival. In such a situation, they send their children to work under the creditor to clear off their debts. In some cases this takes the form of bondage labour perpetual into lifelong bondage. Poverty and child labour, thus, go hand in hand and tend to reinforce each other in poor households.

Another quarter of the respondents cited large family size as the reason for sending their children to work. In large families of the lower strata of the society, parents are forced to send some of their children to work, for the available financial resources do not allow them to send all their children to school. Only one or at the most two children of these households actual school while other work to support the expenses of their school going siblings and they help the family to meet the day-to-day expenditure.

About (one fifth of the parents cited prevalence of high wage rates as the cause for sending their children to work the relation between wage rates and economic activities of children is direct.) An increase in the wage rate for children normally increases the child work participation rates. When the wage rates are high, even children who are attending schools drop-out and join the labour force.

(Parents of another one-tenth's of the children in the labour force stated that they had sent their children for work as there were no educational facilities in the area of their residence.) In most of the rural areas of India, a significant proportion of children are denied education due to inadequacy and inaccessibility of schooling facilities. Absence of facilities, deprives children of the opportunity of education generally children have to travel long distances to other villages or near-by towns for attending schools. (Parents who are willing to send their children to schools find education more expensive when it involves travelling charges. As a result, parents are reluctant to enroll their children in schools.) (Even if they are enrolled, the inconveniences experienced by children make them drop-out early from schools.) Thus children who have no schooling facilities either have to remain idle or participate in economic activities. As parents prefer the latter, child labour comes into existence.

Actual Child Labour Force Participation and Fertility

The best way to understand and relationship between child labour force participation and fertility would be to correlate the occupational background of the currently working children with fertility Table—6.7 shows the occupational status of the child workers by sex and mean live births.

Table—6.7. Percentage Distribution of Child Workers by Occupational Status and Mean Live Births.

Occupational status	Child workers			
	Male	Female	Total	
	%	%	%	MLB
Bead workers, Handloom weavers, Basket makers, Poultry helpers	33.33 (30)	25.00 (15)	30.00 (45)	5.08 (45)
Animal herdsmen	22.22 (20)	—	13.33 (20)	4.00 (20)
Agricultural labourers	27.78 (25)	33.33 (20)	30.00 (45)	3.28 (45)
Domestic servants	16.67 (15)	41.69 (25)	26.67 (40)	3.00 (40)
Total	**100.00 (90)**	**100.00 (60)**	**100.00 (150)**	**3.84 (150)**

(In this area, children were employed as bead workers, Handloom weavers, Basket makers, and Poultry helpers, animal herdsmen, agricultural labourers and domestic servants.) Of the 150 children employed, 60 per cent were boys and the remaining 40 per cent girls. A large percentage (33%) of the boys were working as workers followed by a quarter of them working as agricultural labourers. In contrast, 40 per cent of the girls worked as domestic servants with another one fifth working as agricultural labourers. A very small percentage of the boys were also working as domestic servants, while none of the girls were engaged as animal herdsmen. The cause for this may be that in this area, animals were taken to the outskirts of the villages which were surrounded with dense foliage, not considered safe and hence parents did not prefer to engage their girls in this occupation.

(All kinds of workers were paid the highest wages followed by animal herdsmen children working as domestic servants were paid the lowest while agricultural labourers were paid half the prevailing wages given to the adult labourers. The children were employed throughout the year. If off season, when agricultural operations were suspended, children were paid a little less than the regular wages and were employed to take care of kitchen gardens watering, scaring away birds, cleaning store houses etc. However, both girls and boys were paid equally.)

The data clearly (highlighted to positive relationship between child labour and fertility.) It may be observed that (the respondents whose children were employed in the least economically useful occupations had the lowest fertility.) The fertility of the respondents whose children were engaged as workers with high wages had the highest fertility of 5.08 MLB while those whose children worked as domestic servants had the lowest fertility of 3.00 MLB. The findings revealed that higher earnings potentialities of children were consistent with higher fertility.

SECTION 2

Perceived Labour Value of Children and Fertility

Another approach to assess the labour value of children is to assess the respondents' attitudes and values attached to child labour. Direct measurement of all the dimensions of child labour is an uphill task since some of them are not amenable to quantification. Moreover, the supply of child labour depends on a number of factors aside from the fact that childhood occupies only a fraction of the life span. Parents may not have children currently working still they may attach greater importance to child labour. Therefore, the assessment of perceived labour value of children may be more realistic than the measurement of actual child labour alone. These perceptions are also meaningful as they are based upon real life experiences of individuals.

Age and Net Economic Value of Children

Children not only contribute income and labour to the family, but also involve expenditure. This net economic value of children, according to economic theories of fertility, bears a close relation to fertility behaviour. Age is an important factor in the determination of net economic value of children. One convenient way of measuring this aspect was to ask the question: "At what age do working children earn or produce enough to make up for what has to be spent on them".

Table—6.8. Percentage Distribution of School Going Children Households and Child Labour Households by Opinion on Age at which Children become Economically useful.

Age (In years)	SGCH		CLH	
	No.	%	No.	%
5-9	—	—	18	12.00
10-14	12	8.00	112	74.67
15-19	75	50.00	20	13.33
20 +	63	42.00	—	—
Total	**150**	**100.00**	**150**	**100.00**

Significant differences may be observed among the SGCHs and CLHs with regard to their opinion on the age from which children start earning enough to make up for what has been spend on them. (As high as three fourths of the CLHs felt that working children in the age group of 10-14 years earn enough for their maintenance. As against this, only 8 per cent of SGCH felt so. More than half of the SGCHs stated that it was in the ages of 15-19 years that children earn economically) followed by another 40 per cent who felt that children will be able to earn his maintenance expenses only after the age of 20 years.

The results suggested that only a small per cent of the SGCHs expected economic returns from children at an early age. For most of them a child should grow beyond the age of 14 at least to be net economical.

Like the production side, it would be of interest to know the response of the respondents to the question about the expenditure on children. They were asked "Do you think that the value of money spent on 10-14 age group of children is usually more or less equal to the value of their earnings".

Table—6.9. Percentage Distribution of School Going Children Households and Child Labour Households by Opinion on the Value of Child Earnings Equalling Child Costs.

Attitude on child costs	SGCH		CLH	
	No.	%	No.	%
Less	90	60.00	22	15.00
Equal	41	27.00	38	25.00
More	19	13.00	90	60.00
Total	**150**	**100.00**	**150**	**100.00**

(A large percentage of the CLHs and a small percentage of the SGCHs stated that for children in the age group of 10-14 years, child costs did not exceed child earnings but were, in fact, less. However, 60 per cent of the SGCHs stated that child costs were more than child earnings at the age of 10-14 years.) The differences in opinion confirm the value of child labour to the CLH sector against little or no value to the SGCHs.

Degree of Importance of Child Labour

The actual economic contribution of children may differ from household to household. Child labour may not always be economical to all sizes of families. Some people may not have living sons or daughters in the child labour ages. While some may not have children in the labour force. Even among the working children, productivity may not be uniform. Apart from these variations, parents may attach varying degrees of importance to child labour. In order to obtain information on this latent feeling, the respondents were asked "how important is the child work to you? Is it of great importance, less or very little importance?"

Table—6.10. Percentage Distribution of School Going Children Households and Child Labour Households by Degree of Importance of Child Labour.

Degree of importance	SGCH		CLH	
	No.	%	No.	%
Great importance	—	—	82	54.67
Moderate importance	10	6.67	46	30.67
Very little importance	20	13.33	18	12.00
No value at all	120	80.00	4	2.66
Total	**150**	**100.00**	**150**	**100.00**

(As high as 84 per cent of the respondents in the CLHs) and one fifth of the SGCHs responded that they (valued child labour.)

(Of the 84 per cent CLHs, more than half stated that they attached great importance to child labour) while the remaining one third valued child labour moderately. Another 12 per cent of the CLHs gave little importance to child labour. Through all the respondents in CLH had children working in the labour force 2 per cent declared that they did not value child labour but were engaging them in work to prevent them from being idle. Though the SGCH did not have any children in the labour force, about 7 per cent gave moderate importance to child labour with another 13 per cent giving little importance. However, an (overwhelming proportion of the SGCH did not favour child labour.)

Although parents may state that they valued child labour greatly, some parents may be selling the labour of their children as it was inevitable while others may be able to substitute for child labour very easily. In order to find out the importance of child labour to parents and to see if any alternatives existed, the respondents were asked, "If children were not doing this work, what would you have done?"

Table—6.11. Percentage Distribution of School Going Children Households and Child Labour Households by Alternative Sources to Child Labour

Alternative sources of work	SGCH		CLH	
	No.	%	No.	%
Hire some one to do the work	10	6.67	110	73.33
Qualified adults could do the work	15	10.00	15	10.00
Adults in the family could do the work	125	83.33	25	16.67
Total	**150**	**100.00**	**150**	**100.00**

The data indicated that (child labour seems to be inevitable for a great majority of the CLHs;) though even a small percentage of SGCH also felt so. (However a great many (83%) of the respondents in the SGCH said that adults in the family could do the work instead of children.) This opinion was expressed by 17 per cent of the CLHs also. The findings showed that child labour was a dire necessity in the CLHs and hence the great importance attached to it as against the nil or little importance given to child labour by the SGCHs.

Opportunity Value of Child Labour

In the study area, there was great demand for child labour and equal opportunities of employment were available for both the SGCHs and CLHs, still child labour seems to be highly indispensable for the latter. This was further confirmed when an overwhelming proportion of the parents in CLH stated that they would have to hire some one in the event of children not working. This potential value of child labour may be regarded as opportunity value of child labour. To measure this value, the respondents were asked to estimate the probable annual cost of hiring alternative help under the assumption that there is no child labour.

Table—6.12. Percentage Distribution of School Going Children Households and Child Labour Households by Probable Cost of Hiring Alternative Help (per annum).

Cost of hiring help (per annum)	SGCH		CLH	
	No.	%	No.	%
Work could be done by adults	120	80.00	5	3.33
Below Rs. 1000	25	16.67	12	8.00
Rs. 1001-1500	5	3.33	75	50.00
Rs. 1501 +	—	—	58	38.67
Total	**150**	**100.00**	**150**	**100.00**

There were significant differences between the CLHs and SGCH in the estimates of hiring help. (For 95 per cent of the CLHs and 30 per cent of the SGCHs the estimated cost of hiring help exceeds Rs. 1000/- per annum.) But majority of the SGCH (80%) stated that adults in the family could do the work while only a small per cent of the CLHs opined so. This is consistent with the findings in the preceding tables. This data, therefore, reaffirms that the value of child labour was very high for the CLHs compared to the SGCHs.

Awareness About Consequences of Child Labour

Apart from demographic implications, child labour carries a number of deleterious implications for potential human resources development. It deprives children of educational opportunities, stunts physical growth, hampers intellectual development, renders a worker unskilled with low wages throughout the productive span of life, affects employment opportunities of adults and the like (*Pant,* 1965). Generally rural parents may not perceive that child labour is injurious to child development; but may believe it as a first step in the making up of a loyal and dutiful child.

An attempt is made here to ascertain parental attitude towards the effects of child labour on child development. Table—6.13 shows statements describing five selected consequences of child labour along with the distribution of responses. Covertly, the disagreement on the consequences of child labour hints at the value of child labour to the respondents enjoying it. In fact, in support of child-work, a few respondents have remarked: "mould a child when it is young" and "bend a sapling before it out-grows".

Firstly, all the respondents in the SGCH over one third of the CLHs agreed that child labour deprives children of educational opportunities. It is, therefore, evident that there was a general awareness about the educational consequences of child labour even among the child labour households.

Table—6.13. Percentage Distribution of School Going Children Households and Child Labour Households by Awareness of the Consequences of Children on Child Labour.

Consequences of child labour	Fully Aware				Partly Aware				Not Aware			
	SGCH		CLH		SGCH		CLH		SGCH		CLH	
	No.	%	No.	%	No.	%	No.	%	No.	%	No.	%
1. Child labour deprives children of educational opportunities	150	100.00	47	31.33	—	—	31	20.67	—	—	72	48.00
2. Child labour stunts their physical growth	130	86.67	22	14.67	20	13.33	57	34.00	—	—	77	51.33
3. Child labour hampers their intellectual development	110	73.33	32	21.33	25	16.67	44	29.33	15	10.00	74	49.33
4. Child labour forces them to remain as unskilled labourers with low wages throughout entire life	125	83.33	31	20.67	5	3.33	43	28.67	20	13.33	76	50.67
5. Child labour deprives the employment opportunities for adults	100	66.67	8	5.33	10	6.67	38	25.33	40	26.67	104	69.33

Secondly, about a third of the SGCHs and more than three-fourth of the CLHs expressed their uncertainty on the effect of child labour on physical growth of the children. This reveals the general ignorance about the consequences of the physical hazards of child labour uniformly in both the groups. While none of the SHCHs have disagreed over the physical effects of child labour the corresponding percentage for the CLHs was 51 per cent. Indeed, a few respondents have remarked that physical labour develops children's immunity to hard work and, therefore, a working child might be more promising than an idle child.

Thirdly, for the statement: "Child labour hampers intellectual development", the respondents who stated that they were aware of this was 21 per cent of the CLHs as against a very highly significant proportion of 73 per cent among the SGCHs. All other respondents particularly of the CLHs did not believe that child labour affected intelligence. A few of them have also expressed the view that "intelligence is primarily a gift of God".

Fourthly, a large percentage of the SGCH respondents endorsed the statement that "child labour renders a worker unskilled with low wages throughout productive life". On the other hand, the CLHs were highly varied in their attitude towards this problem of child labour. While over 80 per cent of the SGCHs appreciated this, the correspondingly percentage for the CLHs was only 20.

Lastly, majority of the CLHs (69%) as well as 27 per cent of the SGCHs have denied that child labour stands in the way of adult employment. They believe that child labour, and adult employment are not competitive but are rather complementary. Also among the SGCHs where all children attend school, it was observed that some children help the older persons in the family.

Of the five major hazards of child labour mentioned above most of the respondents endorsed a solitary hazard namely "child labour deprives children of the educational opportunities" and for the rest of the items extensive ignorance is observed, by and large, in both the sectors of population especially the CLH sector;

in view of the importance to be given to the quality of child population the ignorance expressed about the factors that effect child development points out the urgent necessity of education and other interventions among the general population against the practice of child labour.

Perceived Labour Value of Children and Fertility

In order to assess overall labour value of children an 'index of perceived labour value of children' was constructed by combining responses to four variables as described in the preceding tables. The score for each respondent is the sum of points assigned to each of the responses. These scores have been grouped equally and arranged in four levels ranging from high value (level 1) to low value (level 4) of child labour. The score of this index ranges from 8 to (level 1) 32 points (level 3). The objective of this index was to analyse the relationship between perceived labour value of children and fertility.

Table—6.14. Percentage Distribution of School Going Children Households and Child Labour Households by Index on Perceived Labour Value of Children and Mean Live Birth.

Index level	SGCH		CLH	
	%	MLB	%	MLB
Level I (high labour value)	1 (2)	3.60 (2)	85 (128)	4.60 (128)
Level II (Moderate labour value)	19 (28)	3.08 (28)	10 (15)	3.90 (15)
Level III (Low labour value)	80 (120)	2.35 (120)	7 (5)	3.02 (5)
Total	**100.00** **(150)**	**3.01** **(150)**	**100.00** **(150)**	**3.84** **(150)**

The respondents in the two groups differed significantly from each other with respect to their perceptions about labour value of children. The proportion expecting highest benefit of labour from children (level 1) accounted for 85 per cent of the CLHs while it was only one per cent for the SGCHs. At the other extreme, the levels of perceived labour value of children, the proportion of the SGCHs exceeded that of the CLHs. The SGCHs expected least labour benefits from children as revealed from the clustering of respondents around levels 2 and 3 in the index. The data demonstrates clearly that the perception of higher labour benefits from children among the CLHs was consistent with the earlier finding that child labour contribution was higher for them.

Economic theories of fertility have postulated that economic considerations relating to children may influence family size decisions. The data presents impressive evidence on this score. Irrespective of sectors, (the perceived labour value of children was positively associated with fertility thereby confirming the hypothesis that perception of importance of child labour promotes higher fertility.)

(Consistently, the SGCHs had lower fertility and lower perception of labour value of children.) The results of their study suggest that not only actual child labour but also perceived labour value of children significantly affects fertility behaviour.

Suggestions for Reducing Eliminating Child Labour

Millions of children in India have no time for fun and play. *ILO* (1987) figures reveal that at least 58 million children under 16 work for wages outside their families bearing the responsibility of adults. Experts say that children are at risk in virtually every country in the world. And they argue that children invariably wind up at the bottom of almost all national agendas for political and social action. Yet, within this sphere of universal indifference, the problem of exploitation is most pressing in the developing world.

Most of the developing countries have laws on their books and lofty statements enshrined in their constitutions about rights of children. But without a strong social consensus to enforce them, these legal documents become first dead letters. For these children squeezed between poverty and indifference, the absence of effective protection means being pushed to the very margin of society.

Keeping in view this degrading situation of children the respondents of this study were asked to give their opinion as to 'whether it would best to send children to schools or enter them into labour force'. A large proportion of the respondents in the CLH sector felt that it would be best to engage children in economic activities rather than educating them as against 80 per cent of the SGCHs. However all of them were unanimous in stating that this situation arose due to impracticability of an education system which was not work oriented. They suggested work oriented and economically productive education as remedy to this problem of child labour.

The findings suggest that unless the economic status of the rural households living below the poverty line are uplifted, child labour will continue to flourish uninhibited.

Sum Up

An attempt is made to present the dimensions, causes and consequences of child labour in two sections. Section 1 deals with actual child labour and Section 2 with perceived value of child labour. The first section on Actual child labour assessed only the CLH sector as only they had children in the labour force; while both sectors—CLH and SGCH—were assessed to examine the perceived labour value of children in the second section. An overwhelmingly large proportion of the respondents in the CLH's stated that they had wanted their children to supplement to family income and hence had engaged them in the labour force. A large proportion of the parents wanted their children to earn and supplement to the family income and as such they motivated their children to join the labour force. More than half of the respondents stated that their children worked for ten to twelve months in a year followed by about one third who said that they were engaged in economic activities for a period of seven to nine months. In the agricultural busy season, all the children were employed at high wage rates but during the off-season they were engaged to carry on miscellaneous activities at slightly lower wage rates.

More than half of the respondents stated that their children were paid Rs. 13/- on an average while one third were paid Rs. 8-12 per day. A little more than one fifth of the children were paid Rs. 7/- per day on average. For nearly fifty per cent of the respondents, poverty was the main cause for sending their children to work for wages. Another quarter of the respondents cited large family size as the reason for sending their children to work. About one fifth of the parents cited prevalence of high wage rates as the cause for sending their children to work. Parents of another one-tenth's of the children in the labour force stated that they had sent their children for work as there were no educational facilities in the area of their residence. In this area, children were employed as bead workers, Handloom weavers, Basket makers, and Poultry helpers, animal herdsmen, agricultural labourers and domestic servants. Of the 150 children employed, 60 per cent were boys. A large percentage (33%) of the boys were working as workers followed by a quarter of them working as agricultural labourers. In contrast, 40 per cent of the girls worked as domestic servants with another one fifth working as agricultural labourers. The respondents whose children were employed in the least economically useful occupations had the lowest fertility.

The fertility of the respondents whose children were engaged as workers with high wages had the highest fertility of 5.08 MLB while those whose children worked as domestic servants had the lowest fertility of 3.00 MLB.

Another approach to assess the labour value of children is to assess the respondents' attitudes and values attached to child labour. As high as three fourths of the CLHs felt that working children in the age group of 10-14 years earn enough for their maintenance. As against this, only 8 per cent of SGCH felt so. More than half of the SGCHs stated that it was in the ages of

15-19 years that children earn economically. A large percentage of the CLHs stated that for children in the age group of 10-14 years, child costs did not exceed child earnings but were, infact, less. However, 60 per cent of the SGCHs stated that child costs were more than child earnings at the age of 10-14 years. As high as 84 per cent of the respondents in the CLHs responded that they valued child labour. Though all the respondents in CLH had children working in the labour force 2 per cent declared that they did not value child labour but were engaging them in work to prevent them from being idle. However, an overwhelming proportion of the SGCH did not favour child labour. Child labour seems to be inevitable for a great majority of the CLHs; though even a small percentage of SGCH also felt so. However a great many (83%) of the respondents in the SGCH said that adults in the family could do the work instead of children. Child labour was a dire necessity in the CLHs and hence the great importance attached to it.

For 95 per cent of the CLHs and 30 per cent of the SGCHs the estimated cost of hiring help exceeds Rs. 1000/- per annum. But majority of the SGCHs (80%) stated that adults in the family could do the work while only a small per cent of the CLHs opined so. An attempt is made here to ascertain parental attitude towards the effects of child labour on child development. The disagreement on the consequences of child labour hints at the value of child labour to the respondents enjoying it. All the respondents in the SGCH and over one third of the CLHs agreed that child labour deprives children of educational opportunities. About a third of the SGCHs and more than three fourths of the CLHs have expressed their uncertainty on the effect of child labour on physical growth of the children. For the statement: "Child labour hampers intellectual development", the respondents who stated that they were aware of this was 21 per cent of the CLHs against a very highly significant proportion of 73 per cent among the SGCHs. A large percentage of the SGCH respondents endorsed the statement that "child labour renders a worker unskilled with low wages throughout productive life". Majority of the CLHs (69%) as well as 27 per cent of the SGCHs have denied that child labour stands in the way of adult employment. Irrespective of sectors, the perceived labour value of children was positively associated with fertility thereby confirming the hypothesis that perception of importance of child labour promotes higher fertility. A large proportion of the respondents in the CLH sector felt that it would be best to engage children in economic activities rather than educating them as against 80 per cent of the SGCHs. However, all of them were unanimous in stating that this situation arose due to impracticability of an education system which was not work-oriented. They suggested work oriented and economically productive education as remedy to this problem of child labour.

7

Old Age Security Expectations and Fertility Behaviour

In developing countries children are economically valued not only for labour and income but also for old age security to the parents. People in the developing countries are often heard to say that children are the security of parents in old age.

In the past, most developing nations had more or less a self-contained family economy where old and sick were provided for and the younger generation had a duty to care for them. However, with industrial revolution, the family as a unit of social organisation began to fail in its traditional role of providing security to its older members. The situation in India is no different.

In India about four-fifths of the elderly are living in the rural unorganised sector (non-pensioners). Majority of the aged have been and are engaged in agricultural or related activities. But their meagre earnings are not adequate enough to support themselves. The only hope of support especially for the poor elderly, therefore, is that afforded by children and Kinship groups (*Usha Rani,* 1986).

Owing to subsistence farming and lower standard of living, the landless and poor youngsters in rural areas are forced to migrate to urban areas in search of wage employment, very often leaving behind the elderly deprived of the support of their children often far removed from essential services. This has resulted in insecure future for the aged in the unorganised sector.

On the other hand, majority of the low paid pensioners are also facing financial problems as their savings and pension benefits are hardly sufficient in discharging never ending family responsibilities e.g., education and marriage of children, consequent of their large families (*Reddy,* 1986). As a result, they are compelled to seek financial support from their children. Under these circumstances, the attitude of the children towards the aged in both unorganised and organised sectors is not very satisfactory.

Demographically speaking, the deteriorating economic conditions and increasing insecurity about future, having no other source of saving is resulting in preference for larger families as a sort of insurance for security in old age and in times of infirmity.

In short, old age security value of children is of crucial concern to policy makers engaged in formulating innovative social welfare policies and in altering fertility behaviour. However, old age security value of children is one of the least analysed variables.

Hence, keeping in view of pressing need for additional studies to understand better the problems of the aged in different socio-cultural background as well as the conditions that are generating and supporting large sized families, the proposed study focusses on divergent groups viz., SGCHs and CLHs.

Old age security to parents plays an important role in determining fertility of the population especially in developing countries, like India. In these countries children are valued not only for income but also for old age security to parents.

Demographers content that traditional societies are primarily security oriented and thus the family. The kinship group, and the community are perceived as the major source of security and in such a setting, parents feel that their main source of old age insurance are their children. According to *Simon* (1988) "Farmers expect that the children in whom they invest their money, time, and energy will later provide a return on the investment by helping with the work on the farm/business and supporting the parents when they are old".

This chapter examines the source of old age security and degree of reliance, residential pattern, old age security norm, crisis of confidence about children's support, financial help from sons, parental perception about children as a source of help, index on parental perceptions on children as old age security. Further, these variables were correlated with the fertility behaviour of the respondents in the two sectors. But these findings should be viewed keeping in mind that a direct linkage between reproductive motivation and old age security is difficult to demonstrate because of the long interval between fertility decisions and security to be received from children in old age.

Source of Old Age Security and Fertility

India is one of the developing countries where out of 78 per cent of its rural population 51 per cent has been living below the poverty line continuously over a long period of time (*Government of India,* 1989). Of this segment of the population aged are the most vulnerable as dependency increases with age particularly in destitution. In the absence of public provision of social security the economic value of the child will be greater especially where the parents find it different to make both the ends meet let them alone save for old age.

Benefits to be received in old age have two important dimensions. To obtain information of the first dimension the respondents were asked, "In the light of the circumstances of the aged in your community what means of financial support do you think, you might require when you get old?"

Table—7.1. Percentage Distribution of School Going Children Households and Child Labour Households by Perceived Source of Security in Old Age and Mean Live Births.

Expected from children	SGCH		CLH	
	%	MLB	%	MLB
Help from children	27.00 (40)	3.30 (40)	61.33 (92)	4.02 (92)
Income from farm/ business	24.00 (36)	2.88 (36)	22.00 (33)	3.75 (33)
Savings	14.00 (21)	2.80 (21)	8.00 (12)	3.50 (12)
Pensions	35.00 (53)	2.54 (53)	8.67 (13)	3.08 (13)
Total	**100.00** **(150)**	**3.01** **(150)**	**100.00** **(150)**	**3.84** **(150)**

There were significant differences between the two sectors. Only a quarter of SGCHs (27%) expected filial support in their old age as against more than sixty per cent of the child labour households. Interestingly, 14 per cent of the SGCH and 9 per cent of the CLHs reported that they would depend on pensions and savings in their old age.

Positive and strong relationship may be seen between old age security expectations from children and fertility. Among the SGCH, those who expected help from children as security in their old age had higher mean live births (3.3). In contrast, those who stated that they would depend on their pensions had lower number of MLB (2.54). Among the child labour households, similar trend may be noticed. Those who expected help from children had higher fertility compared to those who did not expect old age support and said would depend on pensions as security. Thus, those who reported help from children as the source of security in old age had larger families.

Degree of Reliance on Children and Fertility

To obtain information on the second dimension the respondents were asked; "when you become old, do you expect to rely for financial support on your children—a great deal, only a little or not at all?"

The Table shows that nearly 20 per cent of the SGCHs expected to rely a great deal.

Table—7.2. Percentage Distribution of School Going Children Households and Child Labour Households by Degree of Reliance on Children for Financial Support and Mean Live Birth.

Degree of Reliance on children for financial support	SGCH		CLH	
	%	MLB	%	MLB
Rely a good deal	18.67 (28)	3.17 (28)	54.67 (82)	3.97 (82)
Rely only a little	15.33 (23)	3.07 (23)	25.33 (38)	3.78 (38)
Did not rely	66.00 (99)	2.76 (99)	20.00 (30)	3.53 (30)
Total	**100.00 (150)**	**3.01 (150)**	**100.00 (150)**	**3.84 (150)**

On children for financial support. Among child labour households 55 per cent of the respondents expected to rely a great deal on children for financial support. Little with another quarter reporting that they would rely on children for financial support. This trend was consistent with the economic status of these respondents. In contrast, 66 per cent of the SGCHs stated that they did not intend to rely on children for financial support as against only 20 per cent of the child labour households. About 15 per cent of the SGCH and a quarter of the CLH stated they would have to at least a little on children for financial support.

The data revealed that the respondents who expected to rely more on their children in their old age had higher fertility compared to others who did not expect to rely. The school going children households who did not expect to rely on their children had 0.41 MLB less than those who expected to rely a good deal. In the children labour households those who expected to rely a good deal on children for financial support had 3.97 MLB and as against those did not rely and had 3.53 MLB.

The findings indicated that reliance upon children in old age was one of the main reason for high fertility. It was strongly and positively related to fertility. More the reliance on children for financial support, higher the fertility. Similar trend may be observed in both the sectors suggesting that economic insufficiency and dependency were the main factors in influencing fertility decisions.

Expected Residential Arrangements and Fertility

Expected residential arrangement reflects the traditional social security system. Living with sons is common in this area, since daughters have to leave the parental house after their marriage as per the prevailing custom.

Majority of the respondents in both the sectors—school going children households and the child labour households (62.67% and 55.33% respectively) expected to live with their daughters. It is interesting to note that slightly more than one quarter of the CLHs (26%) intended to live alone. The Table—7.3 data clearly indicated the son preference of the respondents.

The data also showed that the respondents who expected to live with sons/daughters in old age had comparatively higher fertility than those who expected to live alone. The respondents in the SGCH and, CLH sectors who expected to live alone had 2.75 and 3.65 MLB relative to those who expected to live with sons (3.12 and 3.96 MLV for the SGCH and CLH sectors respectively). The data indicated that in this area, people preferred to live with their sons and in a few cases daughters rather than live alone and this perception of living with children seems to be resulting in higher fertility.

Table—7.3. Percentage Distribution of School Going Children Households and Child Labour Households by Expected Residential Arrangement and Mean Live Births.

Residential arrangements	SGCH		CLH	
	%	**MLB**	**%**	**MLB**
Live with sons	62.67 (94)	3.12 (94)	55.33 (83)	3.96 (83)
Live with daughter	20.67 (31)	2.97 (31)	16.00 (24)	3.87 (24)
Live alone	10.66 (16)	2.75 (16)	17.33 (26)	3.65 (26)
No idea (don't know)	6.00 (9)	2.55 (9)	11.34 (17)	3.47 (17)
Total	**100.00 (150)**	**3.01 (150)**	**100.00 (150)**	**3.84 (150)**

Old Age Security Norm and Fertility

In India people have followed many superstitions, beliefs and expectations. Old age security is the major factor affecting fertility behaviour. An understanding of these factors, apart from helping to reduce fertility would also help in handling the problems of the aged which will increasingly become serious in the years to come. The burden of the Government may be lightened if taking care of aged is popularly believed as a child's natural duty as against the emerging feeling that it is not a good custom.

To obtain the views of the respondents on old age security norm the respondents were asked: "In your opinion, do you think that taking care of aged parents is .... a good custom or not a good custom or natural duty".

Table—7.4. Percentage Distribution of School Going Children Households and Child Labour Households by Attitude Towards the Tradition of Old Age Support from Children and Mean Live Births.

Old age support	SGCH		CLH	
	%	MLB	%	MLB
A good custom	41.33 (62)	3.31 (62)	54.67 (82)	3.93 (82)
Not a good custom	7.33 (11)	3.18 (11)	10.00 (15)	3.86 (15)
Natural duty	51.34 (77)	2.75 (77)	35.33 (53)	3.69 (53)
Total	**100.00 (150)**	**3.01 (150)**	**100.00 (150)**	**3.84 (150)**

There were significant differences between the SGCH and CLHs with respect to old age security norm. More than 40 per cent of the SGCHs argued that filial old age support was a good custom as against nearly 55 per cent in the case of child labour households. Among the SGCH, more than 50 per cent of the respondents opined that old age security provided by children was a natural duty.

On the other hand, 35 per cent of the CLHs cited that providing old age security to the parents was a natural duty of the children.

Among the SGCH, those who felt that depending on children in old age was a good custom had comparatively higher fertility (3.31). Those who opined that it was a natural duty of the children had the lowest fertility (2.75) and others who felt it was not a good custom had a fertility of 3.18 MLB, similar trend was observed among the CLH also. The respondents who felt that it was a good custom had comparatively higher fertility of 3.93 MLB and those who opined that it was a natural duty of the children had the lowest fertility of 3.69 MLB.

This shows that when the respondents, in the light of the circumstances around them felt that taking care of parents was something one has to do naturally did not feel it necessary to have more children. On the other hand those who felt that children were taking care of the elderly only as it was a custom and one was to face severe criticism if a prevailing social custom was not followed (especially in the rural areas), which indirectly means that at least some of the children would be considering the elderly as a burden, automatically preferred large families to ensure themselves that at least one would take care of them in their old age.

Confidence about Children's Support in Old Age and Fertility

Parents have certain degree of confidence in children as their source of old age security. However, today due to increasing materialism and self centerness, there is uncertainty prevailing over the continuance of the mode of security. Plausible demographic implication of the crisis of confidence about children's future support is that it may induce parents to desire more number of children in order to ensure help from atleast one son. In this study an attempt was made to measure parental perception of uncertainty or crisis of confidence about children's help.

The Table—7.5 revealed that more than one third of the SGCHs (35.33) stated that now-a-days children are more economically useful for the parents; while one fifth of the SGCH perceived no changes in the economic usefulness of children 28 per cent were uncertain while 14 per cent stated that children were less useful now. Among the CLH 28 per cent of the respondents expressed that children were economically more useful now while 37 per cent stated that they were less useful.

18 per cent stated were uncertain while the remaining 17 per cent could not perceive any change.

Table—7.5. Percentage Distribution of School Going Children Households and Child Labour Households by Perception about the Usefulness of Children and Mean Live Births.

Usefulness of children	SGCH		CLH	
	%	MLB	%	MLB
More useful now	35.33 (53)	2.79 (53)	28.00 (42)	3.97 (42)
Less useful now	14.00 (21)	3.17 (21)	36.67 (55)	3.85 (55)
Uncertain	28.00 (42)	3.10 (42)	18.67 (28)	3.71 (28)
No change	22.67 (34)	2.95 (34)	16.67 (25)	3.72 (25)
Total	**100.00 (150)**	**3.01 (150)**	**100.00 (150)**	**3.84 (150)**

Among the SGCH, respondents who felt that children were economically more useful now-a-days than in the past had the lowest fertility as against those in the CLH's who had the highest fertility. These differences in fertility between the two sectors may be due to the following—the CLHs, who in general, had lower economic status fully behind their children were economic assets, and thus desired more children with the idea that a large number of children would help the household financially. On the other hand, the respondents in SGCH who were interested in educating children preferred a smaller family as a few will be educated and well-placed children would be better able to take care of them in future. In contrast, the feeling underlying in the minds of most of the respondents in the CLH sector was that children of poor parents in turn remained poor and all they could do was to make best of the situation by having a large number of children who could be engaged in the labour force and reap financial benefits. Thus the perception of higher economic usefulness of children, in the present may have resulted in higher fertility for the CLH and lower fertility for the SGCH.

Expected Financial Help from Sons and Fertility

In developing countries like India parents expect help from their sons in times of need. To measure parental perception of expected financial help from their sons, the respondents were asked: keeping in view the circumstances of people you know, are you sure that you will get financial help from your sons? Are you certain of help or a little certain or uncertain, of help?"

Table—7.6. Percentage Distribution of School Going Children Households and Child Labour Households by Perception of Financial Help from Sons in Old Age and Mean Live Births.

Perception of help from sons	SGCH		CLH	
	%	MLB	%	MLB
Certain of help	50.67 (76)	3.15 (76)	9.33 (14)	3.95 (14)
A little uncertain of help	32.00 (48)	2.97 (48)	34.67 (52)	3.86 (52)
Very uncertain of help	17.33 (26)	2.71 (26)	56.00 (84)	3.58 (84)
Total	**100.00 (150)**	**3.01 (150)**	**100.00 (150)**	**3.84 (150)**

It is evident from the data that more than half (50.67%) of the SGCHs felt that they were very certain of help from their sons as against only 9 per cent of the CLHs. More or less equal proportion of respondents in both the sectors cited that they were a little uncertain of help from their sons. One plausible cause for this may be that SGCHs had high educational and occupational aspirations for their children and opined that well educated and well placed children would definitely be more inclined to extend a helping hand to their parents in old age. On the other hand, majority of the CLHs were daily wage workers belonging to the lower income group and usually set up separate residence immediately after marriage. They with their poor economic status, cannot afford to help their aged parents even if they so wish to. Due to poverty their thoughts are more on the present day problems and as much aspirations for their children future are also very low. They do not value education, prefer to have large number of children whose labour they would be able to sell. Because of the uncertainty of help from sons also, they desire a larger number of children so that at least one will look after them old age.

Parental Perception about Children's Willingness to Help the Aged and Fertility

Parental perception about children's willingness to help the aged is also an interesting factor influencing fertility behaviour. To measure parental perception about children's willingness to help the aged the questions in Table—7.7 No-were asked.

The school going children households and child labour households significantly differed with respect to parental perception about children's willingness to help them. Among the school going children households 68 per cent of the respondents stated that their children were more willing to live with them after their marriage, as against more than 80 per cent of the CLHs who expressed the opposite. Around 40 per cent of the SGCHs and one third of the child labour households (33.33%) stated that earning children were less willing to give financial assistance to their elderly parents. An overwhelming proportion (72.67%) of the SGCH and a negligible per cent of the CLHs expressed

Table—7.7. Percentage Distribution of the School Going Children Households and Child Labour Households by Parental Perception about Childrens Willingness to Help.

Statements	SGCH		CLH	
	More willing %	Less willing %	More willing %	Less willing %
1. How do you feel about children's willingness to live with their parents after they marry?	68.00 (102)	32.00 (48)	15.33 (23)	84.67 (127)
2. How about earning children giving part of their wages to their old parents?	59.33 (89)	40.67 (61)	33.33 (50)	66.67 (100)
3. How about supporting their aged parents?	72.67 (109)	27.33 (41)	10.67 (16)	89.33 (134)
4. How about helping in household maintenance?	61.33 (92)	38.67 (58)	34.67 (52)	65.33 (98)
5. How about looking after you in case you fall ill?	57.33 (86)	42.67 (64)	36.67 (55)	63.33 (95)
6. Attending to your needs	65.33 (98)	34.67 (52)	49.33 (74)	50.67 (76)
7. Serving your own guests and friends	54.67 (82)	45.33 (68)	58.67 (88)	41.33 (62)
8. Providing you with adequate recreation and entertainment	33.33 (50)	66.67 (100)	18.67 (28)	81.33 (122)
9. Sharing your responsibilities (apart from giving financial help)	56.00 (84)	44.00 (66)	30.00 (45)	70.00 (105)
10. Allowing grandchildren associate with you	81.33 (122)	18.67 (28)	62.67 (94)	37.33 (56)

that children were more willing to support their aged parents. 60 per cent of the SGCH and one third of CLHs expressed that children were more willing to help in household maintenance now than in the past. As many as half of the respondents in SGCH opined that children were more willing to look after them in case of illness, serve guests and friends. However the proportion of respondents who felt that children were more willing to provide adequate recreation and entertainment was very less in both the sectors. It was 33 per cent in the SGCH sector and 19 per cent in the CLH sector. 57 per cent of the respondents in SGCH expressed that children were more willing to share responsibilities of their parents as against less than one third of the CLH. However in both the sectors, a large proportion of the respondents, (81% in SGCH and 63% in CLH) stated that their children would allow their grand children to associate with them even after they become old.

The findings suggested that white majority of the respondents in the SGCH had confidence in their children and felt that they would be more willing to take care of them in their old age, majority of the CLH felt the opposite. Uncertainty seems to exist in the latter sector which may be one of the factors resulting in high fertility of the CLHs. This was due to the unsecurity of the parents generated by uncertainty that if they had few children than not even one may take care of them due to low economic status, while the probable chances of at least one child looking after them in their old age was more if one had a large number of them.

Index on Parental Perception and Fertility

The cumulative effect of parental perception about children willingness to help parents was examined by developing an index. This was constructed by assigning individual score values (More willing = 2 and less willing = 1) to each of the independent statements. The sum of the total scores ranges from ten to twenty. Accordingly the respondents were satisfied into two levels. Level—I represents "Low status" (less willingness, between 10 and 14), Level—II represents high status (more willingness 15-20).

Table—7.8. Percentage Distribution of School Going Children Households and Child Labour Households by Index on Parental Perception and Mean Live Births.

Index	SGCH		CLH	
	%	MLB	%	MLB
Low status	28.67 (43)	3.24 (43)	66.00 (99)	4.00 (99)
High status	71.33 (107)	2.97 (107)	34.00 (51)	3.71 (51)
Total	**100.00 (150)**	**3.01 (150)**	**100.00 (150)**	**3.84 (150)**

The above data showed that about three-fourths of the SGCH (71%) were confident that children were 'more willing' to help their aged parents as against one third of the child labour households. This is consistent with the data in the previous tables.

Among the SGCHs those who opined that children were 'less willing' to help had 0.27 more MLB than their counterparts. The same trend was observed among the CLHs also. Those who reported that children were 'more willing' to help had 0.29 MLB less than their counterparts.

Sum Up

The deteriorating economic conditions and increasing insecurity about future, having no other mode of saving is resulting in preference for larger families as a sort of insurance for security in old age and in times of infirmity. There were significant differences between the two sectors. Only a quarter of the SGCHs (27%) expected filial support in their old age as against more than sixty per cent of the child labour households. Interestingly, 14 per cent of the SGCH and 9 per cent of the CLHs reported that they would depend on pensions and savings in their old age. Positive and strong relationship may be seen between old age security expectations from children and fertility. More than 50 per cent of the SGCHs did not to rely on children for financial support. Among child labour households 55 per cent of the respondents expected to rely a great deal on children for financial support. Little with another quarter reporting that they would rely a little on children. The data revealed the school going children households who did not expect to only on their children had 0.41 MLB less than those who expected to rely a good deal. In the child labour households those who expected to rely a good deal on children for financial support had 3.97 MLB and as against those did not had 3.53 MLB. The findings indicated that reliance upon children in old age was one of the main reason for high fertility.

Majority of the respondents in both the sectors school going children households and the child labour households (62.67% and 55.33% respectively) expected to live with their sons. However among the SGCHs one-fifth (20%) expected to live with daughters. The data also showed that the respondents who expected to live with sons/daughters in old age had comparatively higher fertility than those who expected to live alone. There were significant differences between the SGCH and CLHs with respect to old age security norm. More than 40 per cent of the SGCHs argued that filial old age support was a good custom as against nearly 55 per cent in the case of child labour households. Among the SGCH, more than 50 per cent of the respondents opined that old age security provided by children was a natural duty. Among the SGCH, those who felt that depending on children in old age was a good custom had comparatively higher fertility (3.31). Those who opined that it was a natural duty of the children had the lowest fertility (2.75) similar trend was observed among the CLH also. More than one third of the SGCHs (35.33) stated that now-a-days children are more economically useful for the parents. Among the CLH 28 per cent of the respondents expressed that children were economically more useful now. Among the SGCH, respondents who felt that children were economically more useful now-a-days than in the past, had the lowest fertility as against those in the CLHs who had the highest fertility. The perception of higher economic usefulness of children, in the present may have resulted in higher fertility for the CLH and lower fertility for the SGCH. Half (50.67%) of the SGCHs felt that they were very certain of help from their sons as against only 9 per cent of the CLHs.

The school going children households and child labour households significantly differed with respect to parental perception about children willingness to help them. The findings suggested that while majority of the respondents in the SGCH had confidence in their children and felt that they would be more willing to take care of them in their old age, majority of the CLH felt the opposite uncertainty seems to exist in the latter sector which may be one of the factors resulting in high fertility of the CLHs. About three fourths of the SGCH (71%) were confident that children were 'more willing' to help their aged parents as against one third of the child labour households. Among the SGCHs those who opined that children were 'less willing' to help had 0.27 more MLB than their counterparts. The same trend was observed among the CLHs also. Thus the deteriorating economic conditions and increasing insecurity about future, having no other source of saving is resulting in preference for large families as a sort of insurance for security in old age and in times of infirmity.

8

Value of Son(s) and Fertility Behaviour

There is considerable literature showing that people have preferences not only about the size but also about the sex composition of their families. There is a common saying that "a man lives on through his son(s)". The preference for a son is an important factor contributing to the value of children and therefore, to higher fertility and large number of children. Of the various determinants of fertility behaviour, desire for sons significantly contributes to large family size values. This area of research has attracted the attention of demographers because of its role in determining the actual or intending fertility behaviour of the couples. Old age security, financial help, funeral rites, and perpetuation of family name are cited as the most important reasons for male preference (*Ramu,* 1988; *Nag and Kak,* 1984).

Preference for son vary between developed and developing countries, it varies between society and society. Strong cultural feeling to have at least one son is found in a number of groups (*Khuda,* 1988; *Lee,* 1980; *Wu,* 1977; *James,* 1977). *Williamson* (1973), summarizing data from many cross-cultural studies, stated that there is preference for male babies in virtually all societies around the world. It has been found that parents emphasise different aspects which prompt them to prefer sons. In traditional subsistence and agrarian societies particularly in patriarchal societies, sons are considered functional for minimising economic and non-economic utilities viz. sons contribute to the family's economic resources by working on the farm; family name is carried on through son(s), sons are expected to perform funeral rituals; support the parents during old age and are considered as assets in village factional politics (*Arnold et al.*, 1975; *Nag,* 1978; *Mahadevan,* 1979 and *Westoff et al.*, 1967).

In India, there is well-documented strong preference for male babies (May and *Heer,* 1968; *Pohlman,* 1969; *Mamdani,* 1972). Among the Hindus a son kindles the funeral pyre and this ensures the salvation of his father's soul. According to Hindu religious belief the son should perform the aforesaid rituals. *Minkler* (1970) argued that the wish to have one or more surviving sons would naturally encourage higher fertility. The historical experiences in India has shown the prevalence of female infanticide, an indication of son preference. The selection of daughter instead of a son for infanticide lies in the fact that a man needed sons to hunt and fish for him when he was past his prime; it was uneconomic to raise female children (*Balikei,* 1929). In a study in old Delhi, *Minkler* (1970) found that even the teachers wanted at least one son indicating that children are not sufficient unless a male issue was there. *Srinivas* (1977) was of the opinion that the majority of the couples desire for male heirs and the commonly accepted view is that the desire for sons causes couples to have more children than they want. In other words, son preference has positive relationship with fertility i.e., the greater the preference for son the higher would be the fertility. Several studies conducted in India also examined the interrelationship between son preference and family size or adoption of contraception and has found that value of son significantly influenced fertility behaviour (*Lahiri,* 1974; *Nag,* 1976; *Khan,* 1977).

The present chapter examines the impact of son preference, importance given to sons, and degree of son preference among the respondents. The findings were further correlated with fertility behaviour.

Son Preference and Fertility

The birth of a male child enhances the prestige and economic position of the family to such an extent that parents may welcome an additional birth in the expectation that it will be a male birth. Preference for son for many reasons may lead to higher fertility at individual level. Couples with a strong preference for son may go beyond their desired family size. Therefore, it was intended to study the influence of preference for son on fertility behaviour among the SGCH and CLH sector. To assess the importance given to son, the respondents were asked to indicate "how important it was for them to have at least one son among their children?

Table—8.1. Percentage Distribution of School Going Children Households and Child Labour Households by Desire to have at Least One Son and Mean Live Births.

Importance of son	SGCH		CLH	
	%	MLB	%	MLB
Not important	20.00 (30)	2.25 (30)	8.00 (12)	3.32 (12)
Somewhat important	30.00 (45)	3.01 (45)	16.00 (24)	4.20 (24)
Very important	50.00 (75)	3.75 (75)	76.00 (114)	4.80 (114)
Total	**100.00** **(150)**	**3.01** **(150)**	**100.00** **(150)**	**3.84** **(150)**

In spite of other differences, majority of the respondents stated that it was very important to have at least one son. As many as 76 per cent of the CLHs reported that it was 'very important' for them to have at least one son, while similar degree of importance to son was reported by 50 per cent of the SGCHs. The son preference observed among the CLHs and SGCHs was similar to the findings of the cross-national study on value of children by *Arnold et al.*, (1975) who found the prevalence of great son preference in Koréa and Taiwan while it was of considerable magnitude in Thailand.

Cross tabulation of importance of son(s) with fertility showed that the SGCHs with "greater" importance for son(s) had 1.50 live births more than those who gave 'least' importance of son on the fertility of the CLHs was also similar. The fertility levels of respondents in both sectors stating a son was very 'important' was higher than those giving 'moderate' and 'least' importance for son(s). Hence it may be stated that son preference has strong influence on the fertility of the respondents. Similar relationship was found in the studies *Jones*, (1977); *Chaudhury*, (1976); *Mindler*, (1970); and *Nag et al.*, (1978).

Degree of Some Preference and Fertility

In order to measure the strength of son preference respondents were further asked: "If you did not have any sons and kept on having daughters, what would you do? Would you continue having babies until the birth of a boy or would you stop after a certain number of girls?"

Table--8.2. Percentage Distribution of School Going Children Households and Child Labour Households by Degree of Son Preference and Mean Live Births.

Degree of son preference	SGCH		CLH	
	%	MLB	%	MLB
Stop after 2 daughters	25.00 (38)	2.00 (38)	5.00 (75)	3.40 (75)
Stop after 3-4 daughters	58.00 (87)	2.60 (87)	35.00 (53)	4.00 (53)
Wait till a son is born	17.00 (25)	4.43 (25)	60.00 (90)	4.92 (90)
Total	**100.00** **(150)**	**3.01** **(150)**	**100.00** **(150)**	**3.84** **(150)**

Degree of son preference was significantly stronger among the CLHs than the SGCHs. Persistence for sons was confirmed among the CLHs as 60 per cent of them as against only 17 per cent of the SGCHs stated that they would continue having children until a son was born. However, the respondents who stated that they would wait upto 3 to 4 daughters for a son was higher (58%) among the SGCHs too.

Persistence for sons was positively related to fertility. The CLHs who had strong son preference i.e., those intending to wait till a son was born and those who would stop after two daughters and those who would until a son was born had significant differences in fertility from each other. Their fertility was 3.40 and 4.92 mean live births. Thus, the CLHs with very strong son preference had high fertility. On the other hand, the fertility of the majority of the SGCHs (58%) intending to stop with two daughters was lower by 2.43 live births in comparison to those who wanted to wait till a son was born (17%). Thus, the data clearly showed that degree of son preference differentially influences fertility.

Among the respondents, who stated that they would wait until a son was born were further probed as to "why it was important to have atleast one son?" *(See Table—8.3)*

Sons were preferred predominantly for the purpose of old age security among the CLHs. In the present study, 50 per cent of CLHs reported old age security as the major motive for wanting sons. As children, particularly son(s), were the only hope of old age security for most of the CLHs, nearly 50 per cent said that it was 'very important' to have at least one living son among their children. The *Operational Research Group, Baroda* (1972) also reported similar findings of having at least one living son for security in old age. In the other hand 40 per cent of the SGCHs reported 'property inheritance' as the major motive for wanting sons. Family lineage and funeral reality was cited by 20 per cent of SGCHs and 30 per cent of CLHs.

Table—8.3. Percentage Distribution of School Going Children Households and Child Labour Households by Reasons for Waiting Until a Son was Born.

Reasons	SGCH %	CLH %
Old age security	20.00 (30)	50.00 (75)
Inherit family property	40.00 (60)	5.00 (8)
Performance of funeral and other religious rites	20.00 (30)	15.00 (22)
Lineage	20.00 (30)	30.00 (45)
Total	**100.00 (150)**	**100.00 (150)**

The importance of son, therefore, reflects multidimensional values deep-rooted in the socio-economic and cultural aspects of life which differentially influences the CLHs and SGCHs. However, the economic value of children were cited as more important than cultural values for the CLHs. On the other hand, declining son preference observed among the SGCHs may be due to their changing attitude towards value of son which was one of the causes for their lower fertility. Unless serious efforts are made to break the vicious cycle between poverty and large family size at micro level, the fertility of the rural poor is likely to aggravate the rural problems. Further welfare measures and other alternatives for son should be introduced, de-emphasing the importance of son.

Sum Up

In spite of other differences majority of the respondents stated that it was very important to have at least one son. As many as 76 per cent of the CLHs and 50 per cent of the SGCHs reported that it was very important for them to have at least one son. Cross tabulation of importance of son(s) with fertility showed that fertility of the respondents (both groups) who stated that a son was very important was higher than the 'moderates', and 'least' importance for son(s). Sons were preferred predominantly for the purpose of old age security among CLHs (significantly). 50 per cent of the CLH reported old age security as the major motive for desiring sons as against only one-fifth of the SGCHs (20%). Among the SGCHs more than one third reported 'inheritance of property' as the major motive for wanting sons. Degree of sons preference was more stronger among the CLHs than the SGCHs.

This study found two elements to be related to each other regardless of other elements of a partilineal system—Sons were the main source of old age security and they were important to continue the family line.

The finding clearly showed that majority of the CLHs were placing higher value of son(s) and expect support and security from son(s) during old age, efforts should be made to take care of old people (especially non-pensioners) physically and financially by providing organised social security systems and by promoting equal value for sons and daughters through effective implementation of existing acts.

The data suggests that a large proportion of the respondents especially in the CLH sector, those who are landless with very little income are dependent on their children, primarily male children expected to receive help both in cash and kind for their livelihood and old age security.

In India, old age pensions, by and large are confined to a small group of governmental employees, while the rural masses have no social assistance or social insurance programmes expect some old age pension schemes launched by some of the state governments, which are meant for only destitutes. In the absence of social assistance programmes reliance on children especially sons is the only strategy of survival. Many of these people want to stay with their children after fulfilling their responsibilities, such as completion of education of children, daughter's marriage etc. They feel that their only means of support in old age—economic, physical and psychological—are children. This dependence on children for security in old age is contended to be an important factor for high fertility rates. Unless this perceived value of the children as a source of security in old age is considerably reduced and parents assured of alternative sources of security, motivations conducive to small family norm may not be generated.

Given the poor economic situation of the nation in general, reflected in the high levels of unemployment, poverty and landlessness, majority of the elderly would expect to depend on their children for old age security in the absence of any other alternative support. But the crucial question is—would this security to ensure for the growing number of elderly by poor sons of fathers and in a situation where the traditional family system is disintegrating. Since a definite answer cannot be given it may be tentatively concluded that old age in India should not be contemplated with enquanimity.

It is becoming increasingly clear that the needs, problems and insecurity of the elderly cannot be left to family alone. The government and voluntary agencies must lend a helping hand in a big way.

9

Aspirations for Children and Fertility Behaviour

Aspiration is an important dimension of individual dimension. Aspirations for education of sons and daughters is one of the crucial aspects of social change leading to modernisation. Aspiration has been suggested as one of the most important forces which may reduced fertility. In traditional societies of the rural areas, children were seen as a source of pleasure and economic security. As development in agriculture occurs, economic standards of the farmers will raise and as a result aspirations for more schooling may spread. The raising aspirations may increase the perceived cost of raising children, and as a result the parents may want small families. This relationship has been documented by a number of studies. (*Vlassoff and Khuda,* 1988; *Kanitkar,* 1988; *Aramburn,* 1988; *Mueller,* 1975; *Freedman,* 1975).

Raising aspirations, stimulated by socio-economic development, are regarded as having anti-natalist implications. This linkage between aspirations and fertility was aptly stated by *Mueller* (1972). She writes—"the Taiwan study suggests that raising aspirations of all kinds have an impact on the perceived opportunity cost of children, particularly in LDCs, and that perceived opportunity costs in turn affect family size decisions".

The relationship between aspirations for children and fertility is also partially explained by 'Quality-of-children' argument. The basic premise of this argument is that parental aspirations for children's future rise as result of the increase in their incomes. But there exists a conflicts between the aspirations on the one hand and the resources for the other. These parents may, therefore, tend to aspire for a few well-educated children rather than a large number of uneducated children. As such, it is the purpose of this chapter to examine the relationship between educational and occupational aspirations for children and fertility behaviour.

Educational Aspirations for Sons

Education is imperative for people especially as the society develops, because without education the cumulative experiences and knowledge gained on various aspects of life by the past and present generations cannot be passed on to future generations. Not only this, education uplifts the status of a human being, makes him rational and creates awareness, directing him towards progressiveness. As such, data on the educational status of the SGCH and CLHs showed that most of the former had at least some education while majority of the latter were illiterate. Considering that education was very important, the respondents were asked to state 'How much education they expected to provide for at least one of their sons'.

The Table—9.1 revealed that there were significant differences between the SGCH and CLHs aspirations for their sons. Majority of the SGCHs who were mostly educated wanted to give college level education for their son while as against this, the CLHs who were illiterate had very low aspirations for their sons. More than half (52%) of the CLHs stated that primary education was enough especially in view of the present day employment opportunities which were very few. However a quarter of the CLHs as also on third of the SGCH stated that they would provide secondary education for at least one of their sons. True to their form, 17% of the CLHs reported that education as of no use and hence they were not going to educate their children. The aspirations of the CLHs and SGCHs for their sons reflect their present living status.

Table—9.1. Percentage Distribution of School Going Children Households and Child Labour Households by Education Expected for Sons.

Educational level	SGCH %	CLH %
No education	—	17.33 (26)
Primary	18.67 (28)	52.00 (78)
Secondary	35.33 (53)	22.67 (34)
Collegiate	46.00 (69)	8.00 (12)
Total	**100.00 (150)**	**100.00 (150)**

Educational Aspirations for Daughters

Educational status of women in India, especially in the rural areas is very low. Most parents in rural India are not interested in educating their children, citing the existence of the vast magnitude of educated unemployed. Further, daughters are not given high education with the view that they would help the mother in the household chores, and learn to manage the house in the process which was essential as they would be married off at a very young age and would be leaving for their in-laws house. Such views were preventing the parents from educating their daughters. To obtain the views of the respondents, they were asked 'How much education would you provide for at least one of your daughters'?

With respect to educational aspirations for daughters, like sons, the difference between child labour households and school going children households was significantly striking. While a greater proportion of the CLHs desired either no or only primary education for their daughters, more than half of the respondents in SGCH sector wanted to give above secondary level education for their daughters. Further, more than a quarter of the SGCH wanted at least one of their daughters to attain collegiate education, while only 4 per cent of the CLH respondents expressed such ambition.

Table—9.2. Percentage Distribution of School Going Children Households and Child Labour Households by Education Expected to Provide for their Daughters.

Educational level	SGCH %	CLH %
No education	4.00 (6)	22.67 (34)
Primary	44.00 (66)	48.00 (72)
Secondary	28.00 (42)	18.67 (28)
Collegiate	24.00 (36)	4.00 (6)
Total	**100.00 (150)**	**100.00 (150)**

The findings confirm the that when parents have certain level of education, they tend to aspire for higher levels of education for their children. It mothers are also educated, then, automatically they aspire for higher education for their daughters. But no such aspirations were visible among the CLHs.

Educational Aspirations for Sons and Daughters—a Comparison

To obtain information on the educational aspirations, for sons and daughters, the respondents were asked: "would you provide same level of education to both your son(s) and daughter(s)?

Table—9.3. Percentage Distribution of School Going Children Households and Child Labour Households by Educational Aspirations for both Son and Daughter.

Educational level	SGCH %	CLH %
Higher education for son	54.67 (82)	25.33 (38)
Higher education for daughter	17.33 (26)	2.67 (4)
Same levels of education for son and daughter	28.00 (42)	72.00 (108)
Total	**100.00 (150)**	**100.00 (150)**

Apart from the sectoral differences the differences in the levels of education to be given for sons and daughters also was striking. The level of education expected was considerably low for daughters than sons particularly in the child labour sector.

While more than half of the respondents in the SGCH sector wanted higher education for sons, a quarter of the CLH also stated so. Comparatively, 17 per cent of the SGCH wanted higher education for daughters also as against only 2 per cent of the CLH. A quarter of the SGCH and about three-fourths of the CLH stated that they would provide equal education to daughters as well as sons, which was either no education or upto primary level only. What is of serious concern is that even among the SGCH sector, very low literacy aspirations for daughters existed as compared to those for the son.

Certainty of Children Obtaining Education

To obtain the views of the respondents on how certain they were that their children will obtain education were asked: "How certain are you that your children will get that much education; very certain or fairly certain, fair chance or don't know".

Table—9.4. Percentage Distribution of School Going Children Households and Child Labour Households by Certainty of Children Obtaining Education.

	SGCH %	CLH %
Very certain	55.33 (83)	17.33 (26)
Fairly certain	10.67 (16)	12.00 (18)
Fair chance	18.67 (28)	32.00 (48)
Don't know	15.33 (23)	38.67 (58)
Total	**100.00** **(150)**	**100.00** **(150)**

Certainty of Children Obtaining Education

There were significant differences between SGCH and CLH regarding the certainty of their children obtaining education as per their aspirations. More than fifty per cent of the SGCHs were very certain while more than a third of the CLHs did not know what future held in store for their children. About one fifth, and one tenth of the SGCH reported that there was a fair chance and that they were fairly certain of their children getting aspired education. Among the CLHs also one third expressed that there was a fair chance. However only 17 per cent of the CLH were very certain.

The uncertainty that existed among majority of the CLHs regarding their aspirations for children's education was mostly due to their low economic status and poverty. Most of the CLHs were living in poverty and belonged to the lower strata of the society. And they believed that poor sons of poor fathers also remained poor and illiterate.

Table—9.5. Percentage Distribution of School Going Children Households and Child Labour Households by Opinion on Advantages of Schooling.

Statements	Agree		Disagree		Uncertain	
	SGCH	CLH	SGCH	CLH	SGCH	CLH
1. Spread of literacy	78.67 (118)	52.00 (78)	14.67 (22)	18.67 (28)	6.66 (10)	29.33 (44)
2. Securing of better occupation	69.33 (104)	56.67 (85)	21.33 (32)	18.00 (27)	9.33 (14)	25.33 (38)
3. The educated bring respect to the family	65.33 (98)	42.00 (63)	14.67 (22)	22.67 (34)	20.00 (30)	35.33 (53)
4. Educated daughters require less dowry	61.33 (92)	31.33 (47)	17.33 (26)	14.00 (21)	21.34 (32)	54.67 (82)
5. Educated children help other children in their education	57.33 (86)	48.00 (72)	28.67 (43)	25.33 (38)	14.00 (21)	26.67 (40)
6. Parents feel proud of their educated children	72.67 (109)	50.67 (76)	7.33 (11)	14.67 (22)	20.00 (30)	34.67 (52)

Striking differences existed among the SGCH and CLH respondents with regard to their opinion on the various advantages of schooling. Consistent with the data in the preceding tables, majority of the SGCH contented the advantages of schooling as against a considerable proportion of the CLH who were uncertain. However among the CLH sector also, a large percentage agreed the various advantages of schooling.

More than three fourths of the SGCH and half of the CLH respondents agreed that literacy was spread through schooling and almost same proportion in both sectors agreed that education helped to secure better and higher occupational status.

In both the sectors, considerable proportion of the respondents agreed that the educated bring respect to the family, and that educated daughters require less dowry. However smaller percentage of the CLHs agreed with this (42 per cent and 31 per cent respectively). Mor than half of the SGCH expressed that educated sons helped other children to obtain education and 70 per cent of them stated that educated children made parents similarly among the CLH also, 4.8 per cent and 50 per cent felt the same.

However, even among the SGCH, one-fifth of them disagreed that education helped to secure better occupations. Similarity, the respondents in both the sectors disagreed that educated children helped in the education of other children.

A small proportion of both the SGCH and CLH respondent, were uncertain regarding the various advantages of schooling. One fifth of the SGCH and more than one third of the CLH respondents were uncertain regarding the respect and dowry aspects of education.

The above data clearly suggests that a large proportion of the SGCH and considerable proportion of the CLH did agree with the various advantages of schooling.

Schooling and Disadvantages

Considering the present rate of educated unemployment existing in our country, most people are not inclined towards

Table—9.6. Percentage of School Going Children Households and Child Labour Households by Disadvantages of Schooling.

Statements	Agree		Disagree		Undecided	
	SGCH	CLH	SGCH	CLH	SGCH	CLH
1. Too few children remain to help with family expenses	68.00 (102)	50.67 (76)	21.33 (32)	31.33 (47)	10.67 (16)	18.00 (27)
2. Education is expensive	74.67 (112)	53.33 (80)	16.00 (24)	21.33 (32)	9.33 (74)	25.33 (38)
3. Present education is useless and superficious	52.00 (78)	48.00 (72)	32.00 (48)	14.67 (22)	16.00 (24)	37.33 (56)
4. Women need no higher education	40.67 (61)	64.00 (96)	38.00 (57)	21.33 (32)	21.33 (32)	14.67 (22)
5. Parents loose control over children	81.33 (122)	58.67 (88)	25.33 (38)	24.00 (36)	—	17.33 (26)
6. The educated will not work at home	54.67 (82)	61.33 (92)	32.00 (48)	18.00 (27)	13.33 (20)	20.67 (31)
7. Children cannot get jobs even after education	72.00 (108)	54.67 (82)	16.00 (24)	17.33 (26)	12.00 (18)	28.00 (42)

educating their children. This trend seems to be increasing slowly along with the proportion of people citing the impracticabilities of our educational system. Keeping this in view, the respondents were asked, to state what, in their opinion, were the various disadvantages of schooling.

SGCH and more than half of the CLH felt that parents could not control educated children. Similarly more than half of the respondents expressed that educated children did not like to work at home, developing false prestige. Keeping in view, the present day problem of unemployment, very consistently, respondents in both the sectors stated that children could not secure jobs even after obtaining education.

A large proportion of the CLHs were uncertain over all these issues compared to the SGCHs. However, considerable proportion of them, disagreed with these disadvantages of schooling. More number of SGCH felt that education was essential and all these disadvantages were not to be taken seriously especially as education made a person more educated. Smaller proportion of the CLHs agreed with the same.

Education of Children and Expenses

The direct financial costs of rearing children consists of the monetary expenditure of children by the parents for the children's food, clothing, education and other day-to-day expenses. Today, the costs of education are very high and many couples feel that, educating a large number of children is a burden. As such the respondents perception on costs of education may influence their child bearing practices. Therefore, in order to obtain information from the respondents, they were asked, 'For a family like yours do you think that providing education for your children will be a heavy financial burden, somewhat heavy burden, fairly easy or don't know.

Significant differences existed between the two sectors. More than half of the CLHs did not have any idea about educational expenses. This was in conformity with their present situation where in they themselves were illiterate and their children did not attend schools. Only a negligible percentage of the SGCH also stated so. However 45 per cent of the SGCH stated that education was a very heavy financial burden and a quarter reported that they considered education as some what a heavy burden. Among the CLHs also a quarter considered education a very financial burden. Only a per cent of the CLH's stated that education was fairly easy to bear followed by double that number of SGCHs.

Table—9.7. Percentage Distribution of School Going Children Households and Child Labour Households by Perception of Education as a Financial Burden.

Perception of Education	SGCH	CLH
Very heavy burden	45.33 (68)	24.00 (36)
Some what heavy burden	22.67 (34)	14.67 (22)
Fairly easy	18.00 (27)	9.33 (14)
Don't know	14.00 (21)	52.00 (78)
Total	**100.00 (150)**	**100.00 (150)**

The data suggested that education was considered as important by majority of the SGCHs who knew about the general costs of education as against this the CLHs did not feel education as a burden as they did not know about the expenses of education.

Occupational Aspirations for Son and Daughter

In order to measure the level of occupational aspirations for children, the respondents were asked two questions separately for sons and daughters as follows: "what job or position would you like most for one of your sons/daughters to have".

Table—9.8. Percentage Distribution of School Going Children Households and Child Labour Households by Occupational Aspirations for Son.

	SGCH	CLH
Same as yours	30.67 (46)	18.67 (28)
Professionals	42.00 (63)	10.67 (16)
Others	12.00 (18)	16.00 (24)
Don't know	15.33 (23)	54.66 (82)
Total	**100.00** **(150)**	**100.00** **(150)**

It may be seen that there were significant differences between the two sectors. One-third of the SGCH respondents stated that they wanted their son to have same job as their's while another 42 per cent wanted their sons to become professionals. On the other hand, more than half of the CLHs reported that they did not know what type of job they wanted for their son. Only a small per cent of the respondents stated that they wanted their children to have same type of job as they were doing now (18%), professionals (11%) and other types of jobs (16%).

This data indicates that respondents in the SGCH sector had distinctly higher occupational aspirations for their sons as against the CLH sector. The CLH respondents did not seem to expect any formal job for their sons. In other words, the parents of working children are not inclined to substitute quality for quantity of children. For them, the perceived opportunity cost of children was less as there is no expected educational cost of children.

Table—9.9. Percentage Distribution of School Going Children Households and Child Labour Households by Occupational Aspirations for Daughter.

	SGCH	CLH
Employment in suitable occupation	30.67 (46)	14.00 (21)
Helping you or other members of family	10.67 (16)	11.33 (17)
Marriage to an educated and wealthy husband	21.33 (32)	4.00 (6)
Helping her children to give proper education	19.33 (28)	10.00 (15)
Don't know	18.00 (27)	60.67 (91)
Total	**100.00 (150)**	**100.00 (150)**

Compared to sons, the level of occupational aspirations for daughters was very low. It generally appears as though parents in both the sectors do not approve of women going for modern jobs. A large proportion of the CLHs did not have any occupational aspirations for their daughters. On the other hand only one-third of the SGCH aspired for suitable jobs for their daughters. While 18 per cent did not have any occupational aspirations for their daughters, only fifty wanted their daughters to be married into wealthy families with another 10 per cent reporting that it was enough if daughters helped in the household chores. Similar opinion was expressed by CLHs also.

Thus, the data shows that there were significant sectoral differences regarding aspirations for sons and also between sons and daughters indicating high son preference.

Aspirations and Educated Unemployment

The propensity to invest on children's education depends

on the degree of certainty of securing employment for the educated. Our security is characterized by high unemployment rate, particularly the educated unemployment. This climate of uncertainty of securing employment may affect social mobility aspirations for children. To measure this variable, the respondents were asked "As things stand at present, low far, do you think, it is possible to secure aspired positions for your children?"

Table—9.10. Percentage Distribution of School Going Children Households and Child Labour Households by Expected Possibility of Securing Job.

Possibility of securing expected job	SGCH	CLH
Not possible	05.00 (8)	59.00 (89)
Cannot say	50.00 (75)	10.00 (15)
Possible	45.00 (67)	31.00 (46)
Total	**100.00 (150)**	**100.00 (150)**

The above table shows the sectoral distribution of respondents by their assessment of the prospects of formal employment, there were striking differences between and sharp differences between the two sectors. Around 60 per cent of the CLH respondents were pessimistic of securing employment after completing education. In the other sector, half of the respondents were uncertain. However, it may be noted that parents in the child schooling sector were more optimistic than their counterparts in the child labour sector over 45 per cent of the respondents in the SGCH as against one third in the CLH sector were hopeful of securing expected jobs for their educated children.

The data in this table indicates that the low occupational aspirations of the child labour sector for their children may be due to the uncertainty existing in the minds of the parents regarding the possible chances of securing employment.

Parental Aspirations for Children's Future and Fertility

It is evident from the data presented in the preceding tables that aspirations for children were more prominent and higher in the SGCH sector rather than the CLH. To examine whether these aspirations were related to fertility behaviour, as 'index of parental aspirations for childrens future' was constructed. This index covered all the dimensions of educational and occupational aspirations for sons and daughters. This index was constructed by allotting scores to each of the responses. The total score ranges from 6 to 29 which yielded a three level index. Level I represents a low degree of aspirations and Level II a high degree.

Table—9.11. Percentage Distribution of School Going Children Households and Child Labour Households by Parental Aspirations for Children and Mean Live Births.

Index	SGCH		CLH	
	%	MLB	%	MLB
Level I	13.00 (20)	4.03 (20)	65.00 (97)	4.82 (97)
Level II	60.00 (90)	3.00 (90)	25.00 (38)	4.10 (38)
Level III	27.00 (40)	2.00 (40)	10.00 (15)	2.60 (15)
Total	**100.00** **(150)**	**3.01** **(150)**	**100.00** **(150)**	**3.84** **(150)**

The data confirms the hypothesis that sectors differ significantly in their aspirations for children. It may be noted that only a quarter of the respondents in the SGCH sector had high aspirations for their children, where as a large proportion of the CLH and small proportion of the SGCH had very low aspirations. Therefore, it may be stated that the parents with school going children had high aspirations than parents with child labour. The data also confirmed the inverse relationship between aspirations and fertility i.e. higher the aspirations lower the fertility. This trend supports the quality of child argument that larger the investment on children, the smaller is the desired family size. Therefore, parents trade-off quantity for quality. This trend may be seen more strikingly among the SGCH.

Sum Up

Raising aspirations, stimulated by socio-economic development, are regarded as having anti-natalist implications. There were significant differences between the SGCH and CLHs aspirations for their sons. Majority of the SGCHs who were mostly educated wanted to give college level education for their son. As against this, the CLHs who were illiterate had very low aspirations for their sons. More than half (52%) of the CLHs stated that primary education was enough especially in view of the present day employment opportunities which were very few. While a greater proportion of the CLHs desired either no or only primary education for their daughters, more than half of the respondents in SGCH sector wanted to give above secondary level education for their daughters. Further more than a quarter of the SGCH wanted at least one of their daughters to attain collegiate education. More than half of the respondents in the SGCH sector wanted higher education for sons, a quarter of the CLH also stated so. Comparatively, 17 per cent of the SGCH wanted higher education for daughters also as against only 2 per cent of the CLH. More than fifty per cent of the SGCHs were very certain while more than a third of the CLHs did not know what future held in store for their children. The uncertainty that existed among majority of the CLHs regarding their aspirations for children education was mostly due to their low economic status and poverty.

Striking differences existed among the SGCH and CLH respondents with regard to their opinion on the various advantages of schooling. Majority of the SGCH contended the advantages of schooling as against a considerable proportion of the CLH who were uncertain. More than three fourths of the SGCH and half of the CLH respondents agreed that literacy was spread through schooling and that education helped to secure better and higher occupational status. More than half of the SGCH expressed that educated sons helped other children to obtain education and 70 of them stated that educated children made parents proud. The respondents were asked, to state the various disadvantages of schooling. Large proportion of both the respondents clearly specified that educated children did not stay with their parents and very few helped with family expenses and further that education was expensive. More than half of the SGCH and 48 per cent of the CLH opined that education was useless and superficious. Unfortunately, 40 per cent of the SGCH and 64 per cent of the CLH stated that women need to education especially in view of the high dowry demanded of educated women. SGCH and more than half of the CLH felt that parents could not control educated children. A large proportion of the CLHs were uncertain over all these issues compared to the SGCHs.

The respondents were asked, 'for a family like yours do you think that providing education for your children will be a burden'. More than half of the CLHs did not have any idea about educational expenses. Only a negligible percentage of the SGCHs also stated so. However 45 per cent of the SGCH stated that education was a very heavy financial burden. Among the CLHs also a quarter considered education a very heavy financial burden. One-third of the SGCH respondents stated that they wanted their son to have same job as their's while another 42 per cent wanted their sons to become professionals. On the other hand, more than half of the CLHs reported that they did not know what type of job they wanted for their son.

Compared to sons, the level of occupational aspirations for daughters was very low. It generally appears as though parents in both the sectors do not approve of women going for modern jobs. A large proportion of the CLHs did not have any occupational aspirations for their daughters. On the other hand only one-third of the SGCH aspired for suitable jobs for their daughters. Around 60 per cent of the CLH respondents were pessimistic of securing employment after completing education. In the other sector, half of the respondents were uncertain. However, it may be noted that parents in the child schooling sector were more optimistic than their counterparts in the child labour sector. The data confirms the hypothesis that sectors differ significantly in their aspirations for children. Only a quarter of the respondents in the SGCH sector had high aspirations for their children, where as a large proportion of the CLH and small proportion of the SGCH had very low aspirations. The data also confirmed the inverse relationship between aspirations and fertility i.e. higher the aspirations lower the fertility. This trend supports and quality of child argument that larger the investment on children, the smaller is the desired family size.

10

Family Size Preferences and Contraceptive Behaviour

The central concern of communication research and practice in our National Family Planning Programme is the phenomenon of adoption and non-adoption of contraception. The so-called 'KAP—gap' i.e. the discrepancy between expressed attitudes and behaviour—saying no more children are wanted and not practising contraception has often been discussed but a large number of couples yet remain as non-adopters. Despite some encouraging trend of adoption in the recent past the targeted goal now is to provide protection against conception to at least 60 per cent of the eligible couples by the year 2000 A.D. in order to attain NRR of one. It is indeed a challenging task which requires innovative strategies, for the diffusion of information about basic ideas, means, availability, costs and legitimacy of family planning so that the non-adopters are mobilised towards favourable attitude and ultimately adoption. However, when a change in human behaviour is to be achieved on a voluntary basis, the only means available is communication, as communication seeks to inform, educate and motivate people into accepting and practising small family norm. As such any study focussing on fertility will remain fragmented if the attitude of people towards family size norms and contraception is not taken into account. The present chapter discusses the family size preference and contraceptive behaviour of the school going children households and child labour housholds.

Ideal Family Size

Generally, the number of children people consider to be ideal and the number they have in reality is likely to depend upon values ascribed to children by the society, the economic structure of that society and its stage of development. In most societies few couples before becoming parents, plan the exact size of their families based on the costs and benefits of children and on their economic and personal resources. The Govt. of India has been propagating two children as the ideal family size. In order to examine the attribute of the respondents regarding ideal family size, they were asked "In general, how many children do you think an ideal family should have".

Table—10.1. Percentage Distribution of School Going Children Households and Child Labour Households by Ideal Family Size.

Ideal size in India	SGCH %	CLH %
Two children	52.00 (78)	14.67 (22)
Three children	29.33 (44)	38 (57)
Four children	18.67 (28)	29.33 (44)
Five and above children	—	18.00 (27)
Total	**100.00 (150)**	**100.00 (150)**

The over all profile of ideal family size preferences reported by SGCH and CLH was one of small family i.e. less than four children. The mean ideal number of children preferred by SGCH was 2.67 and the CLHs was 3.31 school going children households stated two children as an ideal family while only. child labour households considered three (38%) and four children (30%) as ideal.

An ideal family size for 52 per cent of the SGCH was two children, followed by another 28 per cent who reported three children and 18 per cent as four children. In contrast, for 15 per cent of CLHs ideal family consisted of two children followed by another 48 per cent who stated three children and nearly 30 per cent who reported four children as an ideal family. About 18 per cent of the CLH reported five children and above as an ideal family as against none of the SGCH stated so.

The data showed that ideal family size stated by the respondents especially in the CLH sector, was almost equal to their actual family size. Further, the ideal family size of the respondents in the SGCH was lower than that of those in the CLH sector. The respondents preferred family size was in relation to their perceptions of the advantages and disadvantages of large family size. The SGCH confirming to their views of how difficult it was to rear large number of high quality children were more for a small family size. On the other hand, the CLH respondents who had high perception of economic values from children stated a large family as ideal.

Desired Family Size

The concept of desirable family size assumed·importance in the field of theory as well as in Family Planning Programmes. Desirable family size received social sanction in most developed countries. In developing countries the value of children is high and existing cultural set up favoured large family size. In India, since 1952 Family Planning Programme was trying to promote small family norm in different ways.

In this context, in order to ascertain the perception of the respondents regarding their opinion the children of family, they were asked "If you are just married and could have just the number of children you want, what number of children would you consider as desirable?"

Table–10.2. Percentage Distribution of School Going Children Households and Child Labour Households by Perceived Number of Desirable Children in the Family.

Desirable children	SGCH %	CLH %
Two children	55.33 (83)	18.67 (28)
Three children	32.00 (48)	45.33 (68)
Four and above children	12.67 (19)	36.00 (54)
Total	**100.00 (150)**	**100.00 (150)**

There were sharp differences of opinion about the number of children desirable between the SGCH and CLHs. More than half of the SGCH perceived "two children" as a desirable family as against 36 per cent of the CLHs who perceived "four children" as desirable. It may be observed that another one third of the SGCH perceived "Three children" as desirable, as against 45 per cent of the CLHs. Only one fifth of the CLHs "Two children" as desirable.

The mean desirable family size of the SGCHs was 2.6 relative to 3.2 for the child labour households. The desirable family size as perceived by SGCHs and CLHs was consistent with their ideal family size preferences.

Attitude Towards Family Planning

Control of family size by the couples depends not only on their small family ideals but also on their psychological acceptance of family limitation and knowledge of birth control methods. In this context in order to ascertain the attitude of the respondents about family planning they were asked; you know the modern methods of family planning and their uses what is your opinion about family planning.'

Table—10.3. Percentage Distribution of School Going Children Households and Child Labour Households by Attitude towards Adoption of Family Planning.

Opinion	SGCH %	CLH %
Good	88.00 (132)	61.33 (12)
Bad	—	8.00 (12)
Uncertain	12.00 (18)	30.67 (46)
Total	**100.00 (150)**	**100.00 (150)**

Favourable attitude, generally, precedes the use of contraception. The data indicated a favourable attitude towards the adoption of contraception by a large proportion of respondents both in the SGCH and CLH sectors. While none of the SGCH respondents considered family planning as something bad, 8 per cent of the CLH respondents had unfavourable attitude. Further, about one third of them were uncertain regarding advantages and disadvantages arising from adoption of contraception.

The data, as such, taken at its face value suggests, that in the sample area, favourable attitude towards practice of contraception prevailed. This is a good sign as the attitude of the people towards adoption of family planning ultimately influences their actual fertility behaviour.

Adoption of Contraception

One of the most effective ways to study the fertility level of any country is not only to examine the opinion of the people regarding the use of people but also to find out how far they have actually practices contraception. This is very essential as practice of contraception is influenced by a number of other factors such as knowledge and awareness about various contraceptive methods, monetary and psychic costs of adoption etc. Therefore, in order to ascertain the trend existing in the sample area, the respondents were asked, did you or your wife ever practice, practiced or are practising any method of family planning?'

Table—10.4. Percentage Distribution of School Going Children Households and Child Labour Households by Attitude Towards Family Planning.

Adoption of contraception	SGCH %	CLH %
Adoption	68.67 (103)	40.67 (61)
Non-adoption	31.33 (47)	59.33 (89)
Total	**100.00 (150)**	**100.00 (150)**

The data shows that there were so many non-adopters among the CLH as there were adopters among the SGCH. Nearly 70 per cent of the SGCH respondents had adopted contraception as against 60 per cent of the CLH who had not adopted contraception. About one third of the SGCH also had not adopted contraception. The data suggests that in both the sectors, all the respondents who had expressed favourable attitude towards contraception have not adopted it, indicating a gap between attitude and adoption.

This trend was especially striking among the CLH. Which was in conformity with their high perception of economic value of children.

Reasons for Non-Adoption of Contraception

In order to find out why even some of the couples who had favourable attitude towards family planning had not actually adopted it, the non-adopters in both the sectors were asked to specify reasons for their non-adoption; as this information would enable to planners and policy-makers to understand the causes basically inhibiting the people from adopting contraception.

Table—10.5. Percentage Distribution of School Going Children Households and Child Labour Households by Reasons for Non-Adoption of Contraception.

	Reasons	SGCH %	CLH %
1.	Wanted still more No. of children	19.15 (9)	31.46 (28)
2.	Fear survival of children to adulthood	6.38 (3)	23.60 (21)
3.	Non availability of contraception	44.68 (4)	19.10 (13)
4.	Fear that health will be affected	21.28 (10)	15.73 (14)
5.	Practice of contraception is a sin	8.51 (4)	10.11 (9)
	Total	**100.00 (150)**	**100.00 (150)**

The number of non-adopters in the CLH was triple the number in that of the SGCH of the entire sample 47 respondents in the SGCH and 89 respondents in the CLH were non-adopters, though some of them had favourable attitude towards adoption of contraception.

In the SGCH sector, a fifth of them expressed that they wanted more child as against one third in the CLH sector. Nearly fifty per cent of the SGCH non-adopters reported that the method of contraception which they wanted to adopt was non available at the PHC and the concerned doctor had asked them to buy it, which they could not afford, and hence they did not adopt contraception. Further, one fifty reported that they feared that adoption of family planning adversely affect health and did not facilitate hard work. On the other hand, fear of children survival to adult-hood and desire for more children was cited as the major causes for non-adoption by the CLH respondents.

The fact that some of the respondents in both the groups cited fear of health being affected and that it was a sin suggested that there is need to educate the couples and create proper awareness about the advantage of contraception as a whole for the child, the mother and the family.

Sum Up

The so-called 'KAP-gap' i.e the discrepancy between expressed attitudes and behaviour—saying no more children are wanted and not practising contraception has often been discussed but a large number of couples yet remain as non-adopters. Despite some encouraging trend of adoption in the recent past. The over all profile as ideal family size preferences reported by SGCH and CLH was one of small family, i.e less than four children. The mean ideal number of children preferred by SGCH was 2.67 and the CLHs was 3.31 school going children. There was sharp differences of opinion about the number of children desirable between the SGCH and CLHs. More than half of the SGCHs perceived 'two children' as a desirable family as against 36 per cent of the CLHs who perceived 'four children as desirable. The mean desirable family size of the SGCH was 2.6 relative to 3.2 for the child labour households.

The data indicated a favourable attitude towards the adoption of contraception by a large proportion of respondents both in the SGCH and CLH sectors. While none of the SGCH respondents considered family planning as something bad, 8 per cent of the CLH respondents had unfavourable attitude. There were as many non-adopters among the CLH as there were adopters among the SGCH. Nearly 70 per cent of the SGCH respondents had adopted contraception as against 60 per cent of the CLH who had not adopted contraception. The number of non-adopters in the CLH was triple the number in that of the SGCH of the entire sample 47 respondents in the SGCH and 89 respondents in the CLH non-adopters reported that the method of contraception which they wanted to adopt was not available at the PHC and the concerned doctor had asked them to buy it, which they could not afford, and hence they did not adopt contraception. On the other hand, fear of children survival to adulthood and desire for more children was cited as the major causes for non-adoption by the CLH respondents.

11

Summary and Implications

Off late a number of Researchers and scholars involved in the study of population and population planning, have turned their attention to the concept of Economic value of children, i.e. the value of children as productive agents and as a source of security in old age. The economic value of children in India, especially at the micro level, has been a controversial issue. Researchers *Mamdani* (1972), *Usha Rani* (1988), *Naidu* (1983) studying this issue argued that for a majority of Indians living in rural areas, the economic value of children is positive and that this positive economic value has been a major barrier to the acceptance of family planning. Mamdani, on the basis of his study of a village in Punjab arrived at the conclusion that the only hope of a rise in status for the lower class in the village was to have a big family of sons who would either work on land for their parents and help save money or migrate to cities and send money to parents. Considering the life style of the village, he felt, that it was economically advantageous to have large families.

Similar views were expressed by some other demographers. According to *Ashok Mitra* (1976), a large family is still looked upon as an asset by a vast majority of households in India. However, doubts have been expressed as to whether there is adequate actual evidence to support these observations, *Dandekar*

(1977) expressed the belief that there is no adequate evidence in support of the view that the contribution of children to family income is substantial, or in support of the contention that a child is considered a benefit whose value is great but whose cost is hardly perceived at all.

Therefore, the question—what is the economic value of a child in India—remains unanswered. Unfortunately there are no comprehensive studies which can give us fairly reliable estimates of the economic value of a child in India based on systematic analysis of both benefits and costs of rearing children.

Any meaningful conclusions regarding the link between the economic value of children and fertility may be drawn only on the basis of reliable and adequate micro-level data on the actual and perceived benefits and cost of children to parents. It is obvious that such data can only be obtained through surveys—specifically designed for this purpose.

In short, in order to get a real insight into the economic value of children in India and its relation to fertility behaviour, there is a need for more comprehensive studies with the specific objective of examining the various aspects of the problem at the micro-level, namely, the actual pattern of expenditure on children, the actual economic contribution made by children, how far parents are aware of these benefits and costs, and their expectations about future benefits and costs. The present study is a modest attempt in this direction.

Methodology

The general objective of the study was to examine the relationship between the Economic value of children and Fertility Behaviour i.e the labour value of children and old age security value of children, their determinants and relationships with fertility. Conceptually the study was based on the models of *Leibenstain* (1975) and *Hoffman and Hoffman* (1973). In addition a few other relevant models were also integrated in order to widen the scope of the study. A 'non-monetary' approach as suggested by *'Mueller'* was also adopted in assessing the parental perception of benefits and costs of rearing children. As such, this work is innovative in the sense that both the actual and perceived benefits and costs of children have been examined. The specific objectives of the study were:

1. To collect detailed demographic and socio-economic information from the respondents with special reference to Economic values of children and fertility behaviour;
2. To expand our knowledge on the subject of Economic value of children as a motive for high fertility;
3. To collect data on the perceived benefits and costs of rearing children across the two sectors and examine their relationship with differential fertility;
4. To compare fertility levels and differentials in the child labour and school going children households;
5. To identify micro determinants of child labour participation;
6. To assess sectoral differences in the perceived labour value of children and its impact on fertility behaviour;
7. To analyse and compare the expectations of child labour and school going children households regarding old age support;
8. To study the degree of son preference prevalent among the two sector—CLH and SGCH;
9. To investigate the differences in parental aspirations for children and its influence on fertility.

The study was carried out in the rural areas of Chittoor district i.e Srikalahasthi, Puttur and Chandragiri Mandals. The respondents of the study represented one broad section of the population i.e. Non-scheduled caste (NSC) the respondents belonged to the NSC population namely *Reddy, Kamma, Balja and Niadu.* The sampling unit for the study was an eligible couple in the reproductive age span of 15-44 years, with two or more living children and the last child they posses in the age group of 9-14 years. A list of eligible couples in the sample areas, satisfying the sample criteria was prepared for both the child labour households and school going children households separately. Using stratified random sampling technique, a sample of 150 was selected from each list, representing households from both the sectors—CLH and SGCH. An equal sample was preferred to facilitate comparison between the two sectors. Further, it would help to match the sample in the two sectors with regard to all traits.

Data was collected through personal interviewing of all the cases with a schedule. The interview technique was used as the basic method of data collection as the sample included many respondents with little or no education. A schedule incorporating all the measures of Economic Value of children was prepared and personally filled up the investigator. To improve the quality of the data, a short term participant observation was also adopted while collecting data.

Socio-economic Characteristics and Fertility Behaviour

Significant differences existed between SGCH and CLH with respect to their educational status. A large percentage of the SGCH had higher educational levels. Only one fourth of the CLH had secondary and college level education as against more than half of the SGCH. Among the CLH there were 52 per cent illiterates to 16 per cent of the SGCH. The data showed inverse relationship existed between the education level of the respondents and their fertility. Both among the SGCH and CLH, fertility declined consistently with increasing educational levels. However SGCHs had lower fertility compared to CLHs. Occupational differences existed among the two groups. The SGCH had comparatively higher occupational status with nearly fifty per cent of them being employees. Less than 10 per cent of the SGCH were daily workers. In contrast, one third of the CLH were cultivators, while another one third were daily workers. In both the groups, respondents with higher occupational status had lower fertility. In both the SGCH and CLH groups, employees had lowest fertility (2.62 MLB for the SGCH and 2.87 MLB for the CLH). Daily workers and those engaged in miscellaneous activities had relatively higher fertility of 3.85 MLB and 3.71 MLB in the SGCH groups and 3.97 MLB and 4.16 MLB in the CLH groups respectively, with the cultivators ranging in between.

Significant variations existed between SGCH and CLHs with regard to their annual expenditure. In the sample area, more than three-fifths of SGCH respondents (65.34%) were spending Rs. 12001 and above per annum for family expenditure as against one quarter in the case of CLHs. Both among SGCH and CLH with increase in the family expenditure, a significant decline in their fertility may be observed, SGCH and CLH differed significantly from each other with respect to their annual income. Among the SGCH only 13 per cent of them had an annual income below Rs. 5000 and one fifth had 5001 to 15,000 and about one third (34%) had an income of above Rs. 25,000/- on the other hand 40 per cent of the CLH had an income below Rs. 5,000 and only one fifth had income above Rs. 25,000. The high income group had the lowest fertility both among SGCH and CLH (2.5 and 2.6 MLB respectively) and the low income group had the highest fertility. More than one-fourth (27%) of the respondents in SGCHs had high socio-economic status, relative to only 7 per cent in the CLHs. In the SGCH and CLH, the respondents with higher socio-economic status had 2.50 and 2.90 MLB for those with low socio-economic status.

Socio-economic status emerged as the most powerful determinant of fertility. All the socio-economic characteristics independently also had strong inverse relationship with fertility. Lower socio-economic status, especially in the case of child labour households, resulted in high fertility.

Demographic Characteristics and Fertility Behaviour

Almost equal percentage of women in both the groups belonged to the age group of 26-30 years and 36 + years. Nearly one third of the CLH women were young, and below 25 years while nearly one third of the SGCH women were in the age group of 31-35 years. Present age of the mother was directly related to fertility. It may be observed that the fertility of the SGCH women was lower in all the age groups compared to the

CLH. In the age group 26-30 years, the CLH women had 1.00 MLB more than that of the SGCH women and this difference in fertility continued to increase with increase in age. Among the child labour families more than a quarter were married below 15 years of age and more than one third between 16 and 17 years of age. In contrast 70 per cent school going children households married above 18 years, which is the minimum legal age at marriage for girls. Of this, 30 per cent were married above 20 years. In both the sectors, it may be observed that with increasing age at marriage, fertility decreased. There was a decrease of 1.20 MLB with increasing age at marriage for SGCH and 0.96 MLB for the CLHs.

A large proportion of the respondents irrespective of other differences had a marital life of 11-15 years. Negligible number of CLH (6%) had less than or equal to ten years of married life as against nearly one fifth of the SGCH (19%). The data confirmed the direct relationship between duration of marriage and fertility behaviour. In the SGCH group, the mean live births increased by 0.49 for those with 10 or less years of marital life relative to those with 11-15 years. The corresponding figure for the CLH was 0.45. Many of the respondents were breast feeding their infants. Less than half of the SGCH (40%) and an overwhelming proportion of the CLH were breast feeding their infants. The respondents who were breast feeding their babies stated 1½ to 2 years as the mean duration of feeding and unanimously stated that breast feeding was best for the health of the baby. In contrast, majority of the women in CLH were breast feeding and stated 2½ to 3 years as the mean duration of feeding. The reason for breast feeding the babies was that they had sufficient milk and it satisfied the hunger of the baby. The present data confirmed the depressing influence of breast feeding on fertility significantly. The MLB of the SGCH and CLH women who breast feed their infant was 2.90 and 3.60 as against 3.12 and 4.08 MLB respectively, of the respondents who resorted to other types of feeding practices. More than 60 per cent of women in SGCH were healthy while only a quarter (24%) of the women in CLH reported so. Nearly three quarters of women in CLH stated that their health status was very poor. Of the women who were unhealthy, the predominant cause among the SGCH was Malaria. A quarter of the women in CLH were anemic due to too many pregnancies (4 + children) and malnutrition. In this group too, more than a quarter of them were affected with malaria. The data showed that mothers who reported to be unhealthy had high fertility, in both the sectors suggesting that larger the family size, lower the health status.

Perceived Benefits and Costs of Rearing Children

In response to the various statements covering perceptions on economic costs of rearing children, a large per cent of the SGCH's confirmed that they were very much aware of the various economic costs involved in rearing children as against a smaller proportion of the CLH's. Of the various costs which were mentioned as significant, financial burden of rearing children, in the present, increased financial problems in future and providing dowry for the daughter were cited as very important in a high percentage of the SGCH's. On the other hand, among the CLH's cost of feeding and educating children were considered as very important. The overall trend confirmed that various economic costs of rearing children influenced the fertility decisions. 40 per cent of the SGCHs who had higher perception of economic costs of children had lower fertility (2.83); while 12 per cent had lower perception of economic costs of rearing children and had higher fertility (3.22). The percentage of respondents who were greatly aware of the various costs and stated so was more among the SGCHs than the CLHs. Further, it may be noted that perception of various dimensions of cost of rearing children influenced the family size decisions and fertility behaviour.

Significant differences may be observed between the SGCH and CLH regarding their perception of non-economic costs of rearing children as well as their fertility levels. A large proportion of the SGCH (60-85%) cited that restrictions on social life, determination of mothers health, problems between spouses, less leisure, great mental strain, more physical work, tedious and weary work were highly salient costs of rearing children. As against this 60 to 65 per cent of the CLH's stated that mental strain weary and tedious work, less leisure and deterioration of mother's health as important non-economic costs of rearing children. The fertility of the respondents who agreed with these costs of rearing children was lower, in both the groups. The awareness of these costs arising from rearing of more number of children, negatively influences family size decisions resulting in transition in the values of children and thus lower fertility. The data revealed that the fertility of the SGCH was lower than the child labour households. The respondents among the SGCHs and CLHs who disagreed over the influence on non-economic costs and scored low on this index and had 3.18 and 4.12 mean live births as against those who agreed with these costs and scored "high" on the cost index and had a low fertility of 2.95 and 3.68 mean live births respectively.

It may be seen that confirming to the general feeling that economic benefits from children play an important role, a large per cent of the CLH's (65-85%) cited almost all the economic benefits of rearing children as salient. Even benefits like children are inheritors of property and reliable hands to maintain wealth have been cited by more than half of the child labour households. Almost all the benefits were cited as important by school going children households also, but to a far lesser extent. The findings suggested that parents do perceive that children make significant economic contributions to the family. About 58 per cent and 13 per cent of the SGCHs scored 'Low' and 'Medium' on the index of perceived economic benefits of rearing children. The corresponding figure for CLHs was 77 per cent respectively. They strongly cited a number of benefits from children. In contrast, 29 per cent of the SGCH and about 18 per cent of the child labour households stated that they have disagreed with these statements. Among the SGCH those who agreed that children had economic utility had higher mean live births (3.15). Their counter parts in CLHs had 3.89 MLB. Thus the perception of economic benefits from children was a significant predictor of fertility variations.

Among the SGCHs, 60 to 80 per cent of the respondents

cited most of the non-economic benefits of rearing children as significant kinship relation, family lineage and continuity, funeral rites extension social relations, pride in children accomplishments were said to be very important. In the CLH's all the costs were stated as salient by more than 65 per cent of the respondents. The CLHs, in general, had higher fertility that the SGCHs. However within the groups, those who perceived higher non-economic benefits from children had higher fertility. Strong positive relationships between fertility and non-economic values of children may be observed in both the groups. More than half of the SGCH (52) scored low on the benefit index relative to 26 per cent of the CLH. Relatively 42 per cent of the SGCH and 64 per cent of CLH had scored high on the index on perceived non-economic benefits of children. The mean live births of the SGCHs who agreed with these perceived non-economic benefits and scored 'high' on this index was 3.14 as against CLHs who had 3.91 MLBs. Both SGCH and CLHs who did not agree these perceived benefits and scored 'Low' on this index had a lower fertility of 2.84 and 3.67 mean live births respectively.

The SGCHs and CLHs differed significantly in relation to their perceptions on all the aspects of benefits and costs of rearing children. Majority of the SGCHs scored 'high' on the indices of economic and non-economic costs and 'low' on the indices of economic and non-economic benefits of rearing children, and thus had lower fertility relative to the CLHs. This may be due to better socio-economic status levels of the SGCHs which may have influenced their attitude towards various values of children, rationalising their fertility decisions to have a small number of high quality children.

Thus, it is clear from the evidence provided by this study that various costs of rearing children have negative and various benefits have positive influences on the fertility behaviour of the couples. Hence, government should take steps to improve the socio-economic status levels of the rural households through effective implementation of rural development programmes. It should further emphasis the quality of the child in relation to small family size and increase the awareness of people that a few well educated and well placed children will be better able to realize the hopes of the parents.

Child Labour and Fertility Behaviour

An attempt is made to present the dimensions, causes and consequences of child labour in two sections. Section 1 deals with actual child labour and Section 2 with perceived value of child labour. The first section on actual child labour assessed only the CLH sector as only they had children in the labour force; while both sectors—CLH and SGCH—were assessed to examine the perceived labour value of children in the second section. (An overwhelming large proportion of the respondents in the CLH's stated that they had wanted their children to supplement to family income and hence had engaged them in the labour force.) A large proportion of the parents wanted their children to earn and supplement to the family income and as such they motivated their children to join the labour force. (More than half of the respondents stated that their children worked for ten to twelve months in a year followed by about one third who said that they were engaged in economic activities for a period of seven to nine months.) In the agricultural busy season, all the children were employed at high wage rates but during the off-season they were engaged to carry on miscellaneous activities at slightly lower wage rates.

(More than half of the respondents stated that their children were paid Rs. 13/- on an average while one third were paid Rs. 8-12 per day. A little more than one fifth of the children were paid Rs. 7/- per day on average. For nearly fifty per cent of the respondents, poverty was the main cause for sending their children to work for wages.) Another quarter of the respondents cited large family size as the reason for sending their children to work. About one fifth of the parents cited prevalence of high wage rates as the cause for sending their children to work. Parents of another one-tenth's of the children in the labour force stated that they had sent their children for work as there were no educational facilities in the area of their residence. In this area, children were employed as bead workers, Handloom weavers,

Basket makers, and Poultry helpers, animal herdsmen, agricultural labourers and domestic servants. Of the 150 children employed, 60 per cent of boys. A large percentage (33%) of the boys were working as workers followed by a quarter of them working as agricultural labourers. In contrast, 40 per cent of the girls worked as domestic servants with another one fifth working as agricultural labourers. (The respondents whose children were employed in the least economically useful occupations had the lowest fertility. The fertility of the respondents whose children were engaged as workers with high wages had the highest fertility of 5.08 MLB while those whose children worked as domestic servants had the lowest fertility of 3.00 MLB.)

Another approach to assess the labour value of children is to assess the respondents' attitudes and values attached to child labour. (As high as three fourths of the CLHs felt that working children in the age group of 10-14 years earn enough for their maintenance.) As against this, only 8 per cent of SGCH felt so. More than half of the SGCHs stated that it was in the ages of 15-19 years that children earn economically. A large percentage of the CLHs stated that for children in the age group of 10-14 years, child costs did not exceed child earnings but were; infact, less. (However, 60 per cent of the SGCHs stated that child costs were more than child earnings at the age of 10-14 years.) As high as 84 per cent of the respondents in the CLHs respondents in the CLHs responded that they valued child labour. Though all the respondents in CLH had children working in the labour force 2 per cent declared that they did not value child labour but were engaging them in work to prevent them from being idle. However, an overwhelming proportion of the SGCH did not favour child labour. Child labour seems to be inevitable for a great majority of the CLHs; though even a small percentage of SGCH also felt so. However a great many (83%) of the respondents in the SGCH said that adults in the family could do the work instead of children. (Child labour was a dire necessity in the CLHs and hence the great importance attached to it.)

(For 95 per cent of the CLHs and 30 per cent of the SGCHs the estimated cost of hiring help exceeds Rs. 1000/- per annum. But majority of the SGCHs (80%) stated that adults in the family could do the work while only a small per cent of the CLHs opined so.) An attempts is made here to ascertain parental attitude towards the effects of child labour on child development. The disagreement on the consequences of child labour hints at the value of child labour to the respondents enjoying it. All the respondents in the SGCH and over one third of the CLHs agreed that child labour deprives children of educational opportunities. About a third of the SGCHs and more than three fourths of the CLHs have expressed their uncertainty on the effect of child labour on physical growth of the children. For the statement: "child labour hampers intellectual development", the respondents who stated that they were aware of this was 21 per cent of the CLHs as against a very highly significant proportion of 73 per cent among the SGCHs. A large percentage of the SGCH respondents endorsed the statement that "child labour renders a worker unskilled with low wages throughout productive life". Majority of the CLHs (69%) was well as 27 per cent of the SGCHs have denied that child labour stands in the way of adult employment. Irrespective of sectors, (the perceived labour value of children was positively associated with fertility thereby confirming the hypothesis that perception of importance of child labour promotes higher fertility. A large proportion of the respondents in the CLH sector felt that it would be best to engage children in economic activities rather than educating them as against 80 per cent of the SGCHs. However, all of them were unanimous in stating that this situation arose due to impracticability of an education system which was not work-oriented. They suggested work oriented and economically productive education as remedy to this problem of child labour.)

Old Age Security Expectations and Fertility Behaviour

The deteriorating economic conditions and increasing insecurity about future, having no other of saving is resulting in preference for larger families as a sort of insurance for security in old age in times of infirmity. There were significant differences between the two sectors. Only a quarter of the SGCHs (27%) expected filial support in their old age as against more than sixty per cent of the child labour households. Interestingly, 14 per cent of the SGCH and 9 per cent of the CLHs reported that they would depend on pensions and savings in their old age. Positive and strong relationship may be seen between old age security expectations from children and fertility. More than 50 per cent of the SGCHs did not to rely on children for financial support. Among child labour households 55 per cent of the respondents expected to rely a great deal on children for financial support. Little with another quarter reporting that they would rely a little on children. The data revealed the school going children households who did not expect to only on their children had 0.41 MLB less than those who expected to rely a good deal. In the child labour households those who expected to rely a good deal on children for financial support had 3.97 MLB and as against those did not had 3.53 MLB. The findings indicated that reliance upon children in old age was one of the main reason for high fertility.

Majority of the respondents in both the sectors school going children households and the child labour households (62.67% and 55.33% respectively) expected to live with their sons. However among the SGCHs one-fifth (20%) expected to live with daughters. The data also showed that the respondents who expected to live with sons/daughters in old age had comparatively higher fertility than those who expected to live alone. There were significant differences between the SGCH and CLHs with respect to old age security norm. More than 40 per cent of the SGCHs argued that filial old age support was a good custom as against nearly 55 per cent in the case of child labour households. Among the SGCH, more than 50 per cent of the respondents opined that old age security provided by children was a natural duty. Among the SGCH, those who felt that depending on children in old age was a good custom had comparatively higher fertility (3.31). Those who opined that it was a natural duty of the children had the lowest fertility (2.75) similar trend was observed among the CLH also. More than one third of the SGCHs (35.33). stated that now-a-days children are more economically useful for the parents. Among the CLH 28 per cent of the respondents expressed that children were economically more useful now. Among the SGCH, respondents who felt that children were economically more useful now-a-days than in the past had the lowest fertility as against those in the CLHs who had the highest fertility. The perception of higher economic usefulness of children, in the present may have resulted in higher fertility for the CLH and lower fertility for the SGCH. Half (50.67%) of the SGCHs felt that they were very certain of help from their sons as against only 9 per cent of the CLHs.

The school going children households and child labour households significantly differed with respect to parental perception about children willingness to help them. The findings suggested that while majority of the respondents in the SGCH had confidence in their children and felt that they would be more willing to take care of them in their old age, majority of the CLH felt the opposite uncertainty seems to exist in the latter sector which may be one of the factors resulting in high fertility of the CLHs. About three fourths of the SGCH (71%) were confident that children were 'more willing' to help their aged parents as against one third of the child labour households. Among the SGCHs those who opined that children were 'less willing' to help had 0.27 more MLB than their counterparts. The same trend was observed among the CLHs also. Thus the deteriorating economic conditions and increasing insecurity about future, having no other source of saving is resulting in preference for large families as a sort of insurance for security in old age and in times of infirmity.

Value of Son(s) and Fertility Behaviour

In spite of other differences majority of the respondents stated that it was very important to have at least one son. As many as 76 per cent of the CLHs and 50 per cent of the SGCHs reported that it was very important for them to have at least one son. Cross tabulation of importance of son(s) with fertility showed that a son was very important was higher than the 'moderates', and 'least' importance for son(s). Sons were preferred predominantly for the purpose of old age security among CLHs (significantly). 50 per cent of the CLH reported old age security as the major motive for desiring sons as against only one-fifth of the SGCHs (20%). Among the SGCHs more than one third reported 'inheritance of property' as the major motive for wanting sons. Degree of sons preference was more stronger among the CLHs than the SGCHs.

This study found two elements to be related to each other regardless of other elements of a partilineal system. Sons were the main source of old age security and they were important to continue the family line.

The finding clearly showed that majority of the CLHs were placing higher value on son(s) and expect support and security from son(s) during old age, efforts should be made to take care of old people (especially non-pensioners) physically and financially by providing organised social security systems and by promoting equal value for sons and daughters through effective implementation of existing acts.

The data suggests that a large proportion of the respondents especially in the CLH sector, those who are landless with very little income are dependent on their children, primarily male children expected to receive help both in cash and kind for their livelihood and old age security.

In India, old age pensions, by and large are confined to a small group of governmental employees, while the rural masses have no social assistance or social insurance programmes expect some old age pension schemes launched by some of the state governments, which are meant for only destitute. In the absence of social assistance programme reliance on children especially sons is the only strategy of survival. Many of these people want to stay with their children after fulfilling their responsibilities, such as completion of education of children, daughters marriage etc. They feel that their only means of support in old age—economic, physical and psychological—are children. This dependence on children for security in old age in contended to be an important factor for high fertility rates. Unless this perceived value of the children as a source of security in old age is considerably reduced and parents assured of alternative sources of security, motivations conducive to small family norm may not be generated.

Given the poor economic situation of the nation in general, reflected in the high levels of unemployment, poverty and landlessness, majority of the elderly would expect to depend on their children for old age security in the absence of any other alternative support. But the crucial question is would this security to be ensured for the growing number of elderly by poor sons of fathers and in a situation where the traditional family system is dis-integrating. Since a definite answer cannot be given it may be tentatively concluded that old age in India should not be contemplated with enquanimity.

It is becoming increasingly clear that the needs, problems and insecurity of the elderly cannot be left to family alone. The government and voluntary agencies must lend a helping hand in a big way.

Aspirations for Children and Fertility Behaviour

Raising aspirations, stimulated by socio-economic development, are regarded as having anti-natalist implications. There were significant differences between the SGCH and CLHs aspirations for their sons. Majority of the SGCHs who were mostly educated wanted to give college level education for their son. As against this, the CLHs who were illitérate had very low aspirations for their sons. More than half (52%) of the CLHs stated that primary education was enough especially in view of the present day employment opportunities which were very few. While a greater proportion of the CLHs desired either no or only primary education for their daughters, more than half of the respondents in SGCH sector wanted to give above secondary level education for their daughters. Further more than a quarter of the SGCH wanted at least one of their daughters to attain collegiate education. More than half of the respondents in the SGCH sector wanted higher education for sons, a quarter of the CLH also stated so. Comparatively, 17 per cent of the SGCH wanted higher education for daughters also as against only 2 per cent of the CLH. More than fifty per cent of the SGCHs were very certain while more than a third of the CLHs did not know what future held in store for their children. The uncertainty that existed among majority of the CLHs regarding their aspirations for children education was mostly due to their low economic status and poverty.

Striking differences existed among the SGCH and CLH respondents with regard to their opinion on the various advantages of schooling. Majority of the SGCH contented the advantages of schooling as against a considerable proportion of the CLH who were uncertain. More than three fourths of the SGCH and half of the CLH respondents agreed that literacy was spread through schooling and that education helped to secure better and higher occupational status. More than half of the SGCH expressed that educated sons helped other children to obtain education and 70 per cent of them stated that educated children made parents proud. The respondents were asked, to state the various disadvantages of schooling. Large proportion of both the respondents clearly specified that educated children did not stay with their parents and very few helped with family expenses and further that education was expensive. More than half of the SGCH and 48 per cent of the CLH opined that education was useless and superficious. Unfortunately, 40 per cent of the SGCH and 64 per cent of the CLH stated that women need no education especially in view of the high dowry demand of educated women. SGCH and more than half of the CLH felt that parents could not control educated children. A large proportion of the CLHs were uncertain over all these issues compared to the SGCHs.

The respondents were asked, 'for a family like yours do you think that providing education for your children will be a burden. More than half of the CLHs did not have any idea about educational expenses. Only a negligible percentage of the SGCHs also stated so. However 45 per cent of the SGCH stated that education was a very heavy financial burden. Among the CLHs also a quarter considered education a very heavy financial burden. One-third of the SGCH respondents stated that they wanted their son to have same job as their's while another 42 per cent wanted their sons to become professionals. On the other hand, more than half of the CLHs reported that they did not know what type of job they wanted for their son.

Compared to sons, the level of occupational aspirations for daughters was very low. It generally appears as though parents in both the sectors do not approve of women going for modern jobs. A large proportion of the CLHs did not have any occupational aspirations for their daughters. On the other hand only one-third of the SGCH aspired for suitable jobs for their daughters. Around 60 per cent of the CLH respondents were pessimistic of securing employment after completing education. In the other sector, half of the respondents were uncertain. However, it may be noted that parents in the child schooling sector were more optimistic than their counterparts in the child labour sector. The data confirms the hypothesis that sectors differ significantly in their aspirations for children. Only a quarter of the respondents in the SGCH sector had higher aspirations for their children, where as a large proportion of the CLH and small proportion of the SGCH had very low aspirations. The data also confirmed the inverse relationship between aspirations and fertility i.e. higher the aspirations lower the fertility. This trend supports the quality of child argument that larger the investment on children, the smaller is the desired family size.

Family Size Preferences and Contraceptive Behaviour

The so-called 'KAP-gap' i.e the discrepancy between expressed attitudes and behaviour—saying no more children are wanted and not practising contraception has often been discussed but a large number of couples yet remain as non-adopters. Despite some encouraging trend of adoption in the recent past. The over all profile as ideal family size preferences reported by SGCH and CLH was one of small family, i.e less than four children. The mean ideal number of children preferred by SGCH was 2.67 and the CLHs was 3.31 school going children. There were sharp differences of opinion about the number of children desirable between the SGCH and CLHs. More than half of the

SGCHs perceived 'two-children' as a desirable family as against 36 per cent of the CLH who perceived 'four children' as desirable. The mean desirable family size of the SGCHs was 2.6 relative to 3.2 for the child labour households.

The data indicated a favourable attitude towards the adoption of contraception by a large proportion of respondents both in the SGCH and CLH sectors. While none of the SGCH respondents considered family planning as something bad, 8 per cent of the CLH respondents had unfavourable attitude. There were as many non-adopters among the CLH as there were adopters among the SGCH. Nearly 70 per cent of the SGCH respondents had adopted contraception as against 60 per cent of the CLH who had not adopted contraception. The number of non-adopters in the CLH was triple the number in that of the SGCH of the entire sample 47 respondents in the SGCH and 89 respondents in the CLH were non-adopters. Nearly fifty per cent of the SGCH non-adopters reported that the method of contraception which they wanted to adopt was not available at the PHC and the concerned doctor had asked them to buy it, which they could not afford, and hence they did not adopt contraception. On the other hand, fear of children survival to adult hood and desire for more children was cited as the major causes for non-adoption by the CLH respondents.

Policy Implications

The results of this study are very important and have relevance to policy. It has been generally agreed that both development and family planning should go hand-in-hand if they are to be effective in reducing fertility. However, this balanced approach to population problem is a necessity but not a sufficient condition to accelerate fertility transition in developing countries like India. The main findings of this study that both child labour and old age security value of children significantly influence fertility behaviour help in identifying selective socio-economic policies which would strike at the root of the motivation for large families.

The findings reveal that the perceived costs of rearing children was low and perceived benefits from children was high among the CLHs compared to the SGCHs. The population policies therefore, should aim to increase the costs of children, and reduce the benefits of children. Majority of the respondents especially, the CLHs cited economic values of children as very important. One of the most explicit policies that would reduce the economic benefits from children is universal schooling. All out efforts should be made to fulfil this constitutional directive and the non-formal education programme started for dropouts and non-starters in the age group 6-14 in 1977 marks an important policy measure. However, the success of the goal of universal schooling depends to a considerable extent on how parents value children's education. Since parents education is inversely related with child labour, the Adult Education Programmes may go a long way in enhancing the occupational and educational aspirations of the parents for children.

Further, the findings showed that even among the more modern, dowry and wealth brought by children was cited as important. Social workers can educate them on the evils of dowry and the dangers of sub-division of property and wealth in the case of numerous property. Policy makers should be aware of the various costs and benefits of rearing children in particular communities. It should also aim to increase the awareness and salience of various perceived costs associated with higher parities. These facts, have to be given attention in the related educational programmes. Promotion of small family norm among both literates and illiterates require changes in their values about children. Particular attention must be given to disseminate information to the rural couples about population growth as an impediment to improving the quality of life, advantages of having few well placed children and emerging alternatives to children as a source of income and security accompanied by some element of persuasion. Raising income and standard of living of the farmers through agricultural modernisation may also help increase their aspirations for more consumer durables and farm implements and make them more cost conscious about rearing children. Further, by providing certain gainful off-farm employment to women, by developing allied industries, through self employment schemes and small scale and cottage industries, it is possible to increase the awareness and importance of cost and value of time of women folk in general and as such it may indirectly affect fertility decisions.

The findings reveal that son preference still continues to play a major role especially among the CLHs in determining the fertility mainly due to traditional differentiation of sex roles. The farmers feel that sons are more useful to work in the fields rather than daughters. One remedy is to reduce dependence on manual labour through mechanisation and modernisation of agriculture. Further, the vicious circle between value for son(s) and high fertility is to be broken by promoting equal value for son and daughter, changing inheritance laws and practices and discouraging dependence on sons for economic support during old age. Government should also provide certain privileges to the old people in terms of economic, social, and health aspects, by maintaining old age homes and clinics, in the rural areas.

Old age security was cited by CLHs respondents as most important. A son was desired by all of the respondents. The findings underlie the need for the provision of old age pensions, widowhood, security and other rural insurance schemes such as crop insurance, live stock insurance etc. Government may set up associations for the elderly which will not only safeguard their interests but would also conduct recreational, religious and other economically useful activities.

Since son preference evidently contributes to high fertility, measures that reduce sex preference should forms an integral part of population policy. The most useful policy approach in this area would be to improve the status of women. An increase in the status of women may reduce inequalities between the sexes, and weaken the preference for sons. Higher status of women means higher investment per child. With a given income, higher levels of child investments is possible only with fewer children.

Employment guarantee schemes such as self employment, one job for one family and the like may help raise the occupational and educational aspirations for children resulting in the increase of perceived opportunity cost of children which affects fertility. The best example of this kind is Maharashtra (India) Employment Guarantee Scheme'.

People are concerned very much about the financial burden of rearing children, obstruction to wives employment and occupational immobility resulting from a large family size (4 + ... children), irrespective of their socio-economic and demographic backgrounds. These costs, therefore, should be stressed by the policy makers as a means of reducing fertility.

Population policies should aim to increase the awareness and salience of various perceived costs associated with higher parities. These facts, might be given greater attention in public education programmes.

Information on opportunity costs may be used to increase the actual opportunity costs or to enhance the awareness and salience of such costs. Actual opportunity costs could be increased in two ways—by making alternative activities more available and more attractive or by increasing the extent to which children interfere with such alternative activities. Meaningful jobs for women is one of the major attractive, alternative and there is substantial evidence to show that availability of such jobs inversely effect fertility.

Old age security is one of the important values cited for having a large family. This fact underlines the need for the provision of old age pension, widowhood security and other rural insurance schemes such as crop insurance, live stock insurance etc. Government can promote the above schemes which will ensure the parents of old age security thus resulting in a shift of family size from large to small.

Employment guarantee schemes such as 'self-employment' 'one job for one family' and the like may help raise the occupational and educational aspirations for children resulting in the increase of perceived opportunity cost of children which affects fertility. The best example of this kind is Maharashtra' Employment Guarantee Scheme. This type of programmes will mitigate environmentally determined risks which will have a bearing on reproductive behaviour. Risk-Insurance is an important dimension of economic value of children (*Cain*, 1981).

Differences in socio-economic status was one of the reasons for differential fertility among the CLHs and SGCHs. The level on education, income and other social indicators were very low among the CLHs compared to the SGCHs, leading to high fertility in the former group. Hence, appropriate efforts have to be taken to improve the socio-economic conditions of the people especially, the CLHs. Women's education has to be given top priority and it has to be stimulated through the National Adult Education and other population education programmes.

Since, the parental aspirations for education of their children was having profound influence on fertility, necessary efforts have to be taken to convince the parents particularly in the CLHs group, through adult education and other programmes about the advantages and importance of education for high quality children. Further, provision of increased access to education should be accompanied by some special strategies like mid-day meal programmes, supply of free books and clothes, scholarships, reservations in education and employment, and above all, these programmes must be effectively implemented.

Majority of the CLHs are more fatalistic, have strong belief in density, and are resistant to change which are the traditional values associated with high fertility. There is urgent need to change this fatalistic attitudes and promote rational thinking among them. This may be possible by counteracting superstitions, prejudices, fate etc., through presentation of scientific facts and also drawing illustrations from the lives of successful persons who were once similar to them. They also should be made to understand that hard work is the best way come up in life.

Since most of the women were having very low status, there is immediate need to raise their status in the society. The Mahila

Mandals or the women associations at the village level may be treated as important agencies of change among rural women since they have direct and personal contact with the people. It is necessary, to encourage the formation of the Mahila Mandals in the villages and use them as change agents. Family planning programmes, child care programmes, health and hygiene programmes may be integrated with other programmes of the Mahila Mandals. Fresh awareness among women about their equal rights with men to achieve a higher quality of life may be created. Equal opportunity should also be given with regard to decision making on matters relating to economic independence, sharing of property etc.

Further, most of the respondents conceived children without any planning were thinking that family planning meant only 'sterilisation' and were unaware of other contraceptive methods. Therefore, it is necessary to organise intensive family life educational programmes about the importance of non-terminal methods. Steps should also be taken to remove unnecessary fears and misunderstandings about family planning methods. Further, innovations in agriculture should be widely and effectively differed to reach the rural population especially among the CLHs as farmers who adopted innovations in agriculture may be more receptive to family planning innovations also.

The evidence essentially contradicts the view that parents who perceive greater economic value from children are less likely to recognise the economic burden child rearing represents. On the contrary, the results suggest that high perceived values and recognition of the high costs of children do in fact co-exist. While parents perceive their children as values, both for their current instrumental assistance and the old age support they are expected to provide, they are nonetheless highly sensitive to the economic burden which child rearing represents. Such considerations as the costs associated with rising educational aspirations and so on make parents acutely conscious of child costs. At the same time, in the absence of structural changes in the agrarian economy, children continue to be seen as useful, and as a primary means of old age security. Two implication arise from these observations.

First, it is vital to dispel they myths regarding the instrumental assistance of children. Second, there is a need to stress cost consciousness (which, fortunately, is already acknowledged to some extent), by raising the awareness of the reality of the situation, that is, the importance of the economic burden associated with child rearing. Cost consciousness acts as a powerful means by which husbands' demand for children is reduced, on the one hand, and contraception in enhanced on the other. Efforts to increase participation of children in school, via such avenues as the enforcement of compulsory education and raising educational aspirations of parents, is one way to create circumstances conducive to changing perceptions regarding the instrumental assistance children can provide, and simultaneously increase cost consciousness.

It is clear that education and particularly that of women, and mass media exposure operate forcefully on the demand mechanism by reducing the values associated with children and also sensitising parents to the economic burden child rearing represents. This effect of education operates independently of other economic status factors in effecting the fertility transition. The implication is that emphasis on education then may have a powerful effect on fertility even in the absence of economic changes. From an immediate policy perspective, this points to the need to strengthen programmes for non-formal education, that is adult education programmes, especially among women, on the other hand, and to convey relevant mass media messages on the other. In particular, in light of this study, more attention needs to be given to the content or messages conveyed through such education programmes. Notably, three aspects need emphasis: that old age security alternatives do exist; that children are not as helpful to the household economy as is commonly believed; and that too many children constitute an economic burden.

To conclude the above analysis highlights the importance of further need for complementary programmes of population control that not only decrease fertility but also increase the effectiveness of investment in developmental programmes. Our experiences of the last thirty years of planned development shows that the net growth of income has been just sufficient to offset the net growth of population. The gains of planned development would have been larger, if there could have been a stronger check on population growth. Rapid growth of population has aggravated the problems of unemployment and poverty. One cannot deny the inference that all development efforts will be upset if success is not achieved in a reasonable period of time in containing the growth of population. Hence, the need for viable population policies as the 'value and costs of rearing children' that can serve as effective complements to existing programmes and give us the opportunity to influence decisively the quality of life and strengthen the economic and social foundations of society.

Bibliography

Agarwala S.N. (1970) *A Demographic Study of Six Urbanised Villages,* Bombay, Asia Publishing House.

Agarwala S.N. (1977) *India's Population Problems:* New Delhi. Mc Graw Hill Publishing Company.

Arnond, F et al., (1975) *The Value of Children: A Cross National Study* Volume: 1, Honolulu: East-west Population Institutes.

Becker, G.S. (1960) *An Economic Analysis of Fertility in Demographic and Economic Change in Developed Countries.* National Bureau Committee for Economic Research, Special Conference Series No: 11, Princeton: Princeton University Press.

Blake, J. (1967) *Income and Reproductive Motivation.* Population Studies 21 (3).

Blake, J. and Davis, K. (1964) *Norms, Values and Sanctions in R.L. Faris (Ed) Hand Book of Modern Sociology* Chicago, Rand Mc Nally and Company.

Bulato, R.A. (1979) *On the Nature of the Transition in the Value of Children.* Pavers of the E.W.P.I. No. 60. A. Honolulu.

Bulato, R.A. (1981) *Values and Disvalues of Children in Successive Child Rearing Decisions.* Demography 18 (1): 1-25.

Caldwell, J.C. (1967) *Fertility Attitudes in Three Economically Contrasting Rural Regions of Ghana, Economic Development and Cultural Change,* 15, 217-238, Chicago University of Chicago Press.

Caldwell, J.C. (1976) *Fertility and the Household Economy in Nigeria,* Journal of Comparative Family Studies. 7.

Caldwell, J.C. (1977) *The Economic Rationality of High Fertility*. An Investigation Illustrated with Nigeria Survey Data Population Studies, 31.

Caldwell, John. C. (1982) *Theory of Fertility Decline*, New York Academic Press.

Dandekar, K. (1959) *Demographic Survey of Six Rural Communities* Bombay; Asia Publishing House.

Dandekar K. and Dandekar, 1965, "*Effect of Education Fertility*" Processing of the World Conference, Vol. IV p. 146.

Davis, K. (1963) *The Theory of Change and Response in Modern Demographic History*, Population Index: 4.

Dubey, D.C. Bardhan, A. and Gard, S. 1974. *Fertility Behaviour of Working and Non-working Women*, National Institute of Family Planning, New Delhi.

Easterlin, R.A. (1969) "*Towards Socio-economic Theory of Fertility. Survey of Recent Research on Economic Factors in American Fertility*". In Fertility and Family Planning A world View. ed. by S.J. Behrman et. al Ann Arbor University of Michigan Press.

Easterlin, R.A. (1975) "*An Economic Framework for Fertility Analysis* Study in Family Planning: 6.

Easterlin, R.A. (1978). *New Directions for the Economics of Fertility*, in YINGER, J. Miltin and Cutler, Stephen J. (Fds). *Major Social Issues: A Multi-Disciplinary View*, New York; Free Press.

Fawcett. James T. (1972) *The Satisfaction and Costs of Children Theories, Concepts, Methods*. Honolulu; East-West Population Institutes.

Fawcett. J.T., (1977) "*The Value and Cost of Children; Converging Theory and Research*". In the Economic and Social Supports for High Fertility. Edited by Lodo. T. Ruzicka, Proceedings of the Confidence held in Canberra, 16-18, November 1976.

Freed Man, R. et al. (1959) *Family Planning, Sterility and Population Growth*, New York: Mc Graw-Hill.

Freed Man, R, (1963) "*Norms for Family Size in Underdeveloped Areas*" Proceeding the Royal Society 15g: 220-34.

Freed Man, Ronald (1968) "*Norms for Family Size in Undeveloped areas*" in Reading on Population, Edited by David M. Heer, p.p. 157-180. Engle Word Cliffs, N.J; Printice Hall, Inc.

Freed Man, Ronald and Bernord Berelon, 1976. *The Record of Family Planning Programmes,* Studies in Family Planning, 7. 1-40.

Hoff Man, L.N: (1975). *The Value of Children to Parents and the American Philosophical Society* 119: 430-438.

Hoff Man, LW and M.C. Hoff Man (1973). *The Value of Children to Parents* in, J.T. Fawcett (Ed) *Psychological Perspectives in Population.* New York: Basic Books.

Indian Association for the Study of Population (1979) *Child in India: Resume of Proceedings and Conclusions and Recommendations of the Conference.* Delhi Institute of Economic Growth Campus.

India, Office of the Registrar General 1970, *Fertility Differentials in India, 1972, Results of the Fertility Survey in Sub-Sample of SRS* (1972); New Delhi.

Jorapur, P.B. 1967. *Fertility Study of Dharwar.* Journal of Institute of Economic Research VI (2).

Kiser, V. (1936) Referred in Smith, T.L. and Zopt, P.E. Book Demography: *Principles and Methods,* Philadelphia; F.A. Davis Company.

Kiser, C.V. (1960) *Differentials Fertility Unites States* National Bureau of Economic Research, Princeton.

Kulakarni, Sumathi 1979. *"Economic Value of Children in Demography and Socio-economic Aspects of the Child in India,* Edited by K. Srinivasan et. al., pp. 235-252, Bombay, Himalaya.

Leibenstein, H. (1979) *An Interpretation of the Economic Theory of Fertility: Promissing Path or Blind Alley* Journal of Economic Literature. 12 (2).

Mahadevan, K. (1972) *A Sociological Approach of Raising Age at Marriage,* Bulletin of the Gandhigram Institute of Rural Health and Family Planning 6 (3): 245-260.

Mahadevan, K. (1979) *Sociology of Fertility Determinants of Fertility Differentials in South India,* New Delhi: Sterling Publishers.

Mitra, A. (1979) *Demographic Transition and Future Prospects of the Child in Demographic and Socio-economic Aspects of the Child in India.*

Mueller, E. (1972) *"Economic Costs and Values of Children"* Contraceptualisation and Measurement in Fawcett (Fd) *Satisfaction and Costs of Children, Theories, Concepts, Methods,* Honolulu, Ewc.

Mueller, E. (1972) *Economic Motives for Family Limitations, A Study Conducted in Taiwan, Population Studies,* 26 (3). 383-403 Population Investigation Committee London, School of Economics.

Nag, Moni: (1978) *An Anthropological Approach to the Study of Economic Value of Children in Jaw and Nepal* Current Anthropology, (19), 63.

Notestein, F.W. (1945) *Population. The Long View in Schultzt T, (Ed)* Food for the World.

Naidu, D. Adikesavulu. 1982 *Child Labour, Value of Children and Fertility Behaviour.* Ph.D. Dissertation, Tirupathi. S.V. University (Mimeo).

Rajasekhar, K. (1989) *"Old Age Security of the Pensioners and Non-Pensioners Families"* Ph.D. Dissertation, Tirupathi, S.V. University.

Rele and Kanitkar (1974) *Residence Background and Fertility in Great Bombay.* (Population Studies), 28 (1-2).

Recd R.H. and M.C. Intosh (1972) *Costs of Children in U.S. Commission on Population Growth and the American Future.* Economic Aspects of Population Change Washington, D.C., U.S. Government Printing Office.

Saxena, G.B. (1965) *Differential Fertility in Rural Hindu Community,* A Sample Survey of Rural U.P. India, Economics Quarterly 12 (3).

Schultz, T.P. (1973) *Explanation of Birth Rate Changes Over Space and Time.* A Study of Taiwan (Journal of Political Economy—81).

Schultz, T.W. (1974) *"The Value of Children,* Economic Perspectives (Journal of Political Economy, 81).

Simmons, A.B. (1977) *The Value of Children Approach in Population Policies; New Hope or False Promise?* Paper in International Conference, Mexico 1977, Vol. 1., Liege; International Union for the Scientific Study of Population.

Simon, J. (1974) *The Effect of Income on Fertility,* Chapel Hill, Carolina Population Centre, University of North Carolin.

Sinha, J.N. (1967) *Differentials Fertility and Family Limitations in an Urban Community of Uttar Pradesh.* Population Studies XI.

Srinivasan, K. (1967) *A Prospective Study on Fertility Behaviour of a Group of Married Women in Rural India,* Design and Findings of the First Round of Enquiry, Population Review X (2).

U.N. (1973) Fertility, Chapter 4. *In Determinants and Consequences of Population Trends* Volume: 1 (New York).

UNFCEF (1981) *An Analysis of the Situation of Children in India* (Draft Report) New Delhi: Regional Office for S.C. Asia.

U.N. Population Commission (1955) World Population Conference.

U.N. (1961) *Mysore Population Study*, New York: Department of Economic and Social Affairs.

U.N. 1975. "*Status of Women and Family Planning*" (C/CN-6/575/Ref. No. E/75/V5; 1975) New York.

Usha Rani, D. 1979. *Cost of Rearing Children and its Impact on Fertility*. M. Phil. Dissertation Submitted to Sri Venkateswara University, Tirupati (Mimeo).

Usha Rani, D. 1983. *Cost of Rearing Children and Other Socio-economic Determinant of Fertility*. Ph.D. Dissertation. Sri Venkateswara University, Tirupati.

Willies, Robert, J. 1979. "*The Old age Security Hypothesis and Population Growth*", Working Paper No: 372, NBER Working Paper Series, Cambridge, Mass; National Bureau of Economic Research.

Index